Please Hear What I'm Not Saying

compiled and edited by Isabelle Kenyon

Book designed by About. Design

To my mother and her mother, Maureen

You both deserve a book, at least.

Contents

The reader of this book must name
the sections for themselves

Letter from the Editor

This book has been a labour of love for me. The project started with the simple idea that I wanted to work collaboratively on a project with other poets. I also wanted to do something for a charity and I believed that Mental Health charities were under significant strain – and doing some very important work.

When I first put the word out that I was accepting submissions for the anthology 'Please Hear What I'm Not Saying', I didn't think many people would want to be involved. The sheer number of people in contact with me is a testimony to the work which MIND does.

This book is divided into sections – the idea is that the sections grow with positivity and that, by the end of the book, you will be able to see the light at the end of the tunnel. Therefore, please feel free to dip in and out of sections, and if you begin to find the words too heavy, please do nip straight to the last sections for a breather!

I hope you enjoy reading this book. Thank you for your contribution to MIND.

Love,

Isabelle Charlotte Kenyon

www.flyonthewallpoetry.co.uk
Author of 'This is not a Spectacle';
Micro chapbook, 'The Trees Whispered', by Origami Poetry Press.
Social Media Links:
Instagram: flyonthewall_poetry
Twitter: kenyon_isabelle
Facebook: flyonthewallpoetry

One

The thing that's grown inside me
cannot be explored by ultra-sound,
or removed by surgeon's knife.

I go to work as normal.
It exists inside my gut
and mind: controlling.

To leave the house in haste cannot be done.
First I feed the gnawing devil with ritual;
kettle, cooker, lights, taps,
switches, back-door. Kettle, cooker,
lights, taps, switches, back-door.

It wants more.
Plaster cracking is subsidence,
unknown emails contain viruses.
I cannot pay by phone
or order online just in case.

Awake at night to the electric thrum,
sweating to think of what comes next.
No scan can show this demon.
No lump can be removed.

Invisible
By Neil Elder

Mental illness
is a battle I never agreed to fight.

A silent war,
where the enemy tactic
is to try to convince you
that the war
isn't happening
at all.

But I've seen the bodies,
I've seen the blood,
I've fought the battleground,
I've bandaged the bullet wounds.

And after all, I'm surviving.
I promise, I will receive my medal.

Battle
By Bethany Gordon

Unwelcome guest
who arrives without warning
and has to be accommodated.
Has the fussiest needs,
won't eat meals,
snacks on chocolate,
disturbs sleep,
shows no interest
in outings;
occupies the best chair.

Leaves without warning
one fine day,
no word
of thanks or goodbye;
will be back one day
when least expected.

Depression
By Angela Topping

Is a rainy afternoon in a small Northern town,
a cold coffee in a polystyrene cup,
an empty bus stationary at the roadside,
a browned apple core lying in the gutter.
It's one note adrift from its score
or sounding itself in the wrong piece of music,
a ready-meal for one on Christmas day.
Is waiting for anyone to find it.

Loneliness
By Angela Topping

Grief is a cruel handbag -
its catch snaps shut like jaws.
Inside is buried an old compact,
hankie embroidered with an M
in a huddle of forget-me-nots.
There's a used-up biro, one cherry lipstick,
a purse stained from long-dead hands,
inside only a few pence, a stamp.
The handbag is a stomach
digesting the past. What can be
done with it? It cannot be thrown away.
Best hide it in the bottom of the wardrobe
an unexploded bomb.

Deferment
By Angela Topping

She brought you to bingo
to slice through numbers
with a black marker
on Monday nights
to keep you sober
and from the vodka slumber.

For company,
for your own safety,
to keep you out
of the kitchen drawer
and the cold, blue bathroom
that didn't have a key.

You collected the bottles
maintained your nails and
highlights, everything else
on a landslide, slid away
and your only break
from those four yellow walls
 was into a big book
and two fat ladies.

Legs Eleven
By Lorraine Carey

The wolf whistles pierced
pensioner concentration
in the musty parish hall.
Kelly's Eye, key of the door,
and all the others.
The call lodged in throats
waited to rise and shout,
the black slashes
marked a full house.

A sneaky trip for mouthwash,
then back to front seat denial
and another bag search.
The yellow walls heard
the coughs to muffle the breaking seal,
the broken spiral of a new litre
to where it all went wrong.

Previously published in Issue 10 of The Blue Nib (August 2017)

Muriel laughs at life,
She's made of sunbeams,
Shiny, happy people
Inhabit her dreams

Maud weeps at life,
A crumpling heap,
Fearsome ravenous monsters
Haunt her sleep

Muriel comes out to play,
Runs to hug the trees.
She makes a fragrant garden
For the fur-backed bees

Maud cowers at home,
Outdoors is noise and litter,
It's a daily struggle
Not to turn bitter

I am both Maud and Muriel
By equal turns;
Anyone who draws near
Soon learns.

Two Women
By Jan McCarthy

Last night

I baked her
a thought-cake.

Today

she at
last opened her
lips
nibbled the
few
crumbs I
offered from
my tongue.

Now

through the bathroom door
the heave and flush.

Ana's Therapy, Day 168
By Jinny Fisher

an amorphous cloud encroaches
as you struggle to carry on

everything seems out of kilter
you sense there is something wrong

you are trying not to listen
to the sibilance of depression

hissing in your ears
interfering with your thoughts

filling you with fears
yet depression is snaking around you

constricting every breath
its viper-grip deflating you

ripping off the plaster you repaired
the last puncture with

exhausting all resistance
inviting depths of gloominess

to take root inside your chest
installing a chasm of lonely emptiness

and still you try to block it
by stepping up for the fight

trying to re-inflate yourself
before the fog obscures the light

The Sibilance of Depression
By CR Smith

Oh and I want to spill to you all the secrets of my fishy
heart and tell you my damage and let you see what it's done
to me, so you can smile and take me by the hand

echo my chlorine rinse, swimming in the same blue water
as me, and tell me it's ok, so that I want, what I always want,
which is to kiss you on your lovely mouth and walk

with you arm in arm, goggle eyed and wincing
in the cold, so we go into a candlelit bar and order sloe gin
and let it slip down inside us, feeling the warmth

spreading into us, steaming our wet locks of hair and we talk
in low voices and giggle and grab hold and walk out into the snow
of each other's hearts, throwing handfuls of pain at each other

but it doesn't matter at all because there's no work tomorrow
or if there is, we're gonna call in sick, so we can float home
together and talk all night and lie down sobbing

in each other's arms and everything will be ok
when we're catching each other's eyes and laughing
at the world that can't understand us because we refuse

to conform to the niceties asked of us and we laugh
and laugh at the phone, because it won't stop ringing
but then I want to turn back the clock and unsay some

of the things we've been saying to each other
in case we've actually only imagined being understood
and in turning back I could say to you the things

For the Swimmers
By Sarah Wallis

I really want to say that usually stay locked up inside my head
filling a swimming pool sized lake in my mind with blue
lagoonary, visions of summer days we've never known, by the lido,

by the lido, I am awash with my dreams with you in my arms
and I want to sit down in the park and plait daisies into your hair
like I did with my friends when I was that young, when we were

five or six years old and could giggle all day long for the sheer
pleasure of being together when your best friend made you feel
light and dizzy and jellylegs and cared for and fizzy

like you ate a bellyful of sherbet, or packets and packets
of refreshers and parma violets, remember being that giggly
with sugar rush, with fierce love, like you are five

or seven again... except, I was never that child. Too serious.

Kids that experience trauma early on miss the giggly stage.
What they do instead is watch. Learn to swim. Observe.
And this un-nerves everyone. So they learn to imitate.

Good little fish in a little glass pool, swimming with content.
Mimic a good time,
and carry their damage lightly, as lightly, as they possibly can.

I once loved something dark,
It was small and pointy,
It parted its hair in peculiar ways
And that was one of the first things
That I fixed.
It came out of the dark
For a moment to offer me
Solace, and promise eternal happiness
Starting in the back seat of a car.

It wanted more than I could give
At a young and innocent time,
I was not ripe or interesting
Or as plentiful as I am today

But the dark thing wanted even less of me,
Wanted to carve me out,
Wanted to reel me in

The dark thing with ugly eyes
(The only ugly eyes I've even seen)
Flattened me into paper
And I've had to write myself out
Ever since.

I Once Loved Something Dark
By Miriam Calleja

I am wired
By palsied hands,
Working from an out of date
Circuit plan
I was bright eyed once
A lighthouse
Of shifting colours
But sometimes now
I disconnect
Overloaded
And bared
My copper
Is mined
Too deep
In the dark,
And I spark
As positive
And negative
Do battle
I cannot find
An earth
To put my skin on
Even with my
Face pressed into the dirt
This electricity
It burns
It hurts,
As people
Far away watch
The pretty lightning

WIRED
By Barry Fentiman Hall

She has given up.
Given in.
The dragging ache of wanting just to lie all day,
the curtains shut against the sharp and glare of people's view.
So she has given in -
The social dainties, wash and dress and keep the house
are secondary now
to sloth and greed,
she'll have them all
except for lust.

A jug for pissing in;
a warm and soiled blanket.
This is how she'll live,
supine on the couch
in the oblong sun,
reaching for another fag.
Life has narrowed to the run
from kitchen sink to couch,

She Has Given Up
By Rachel McGladdery

everything else remote and senseless,
the phone barks accusations so she snips the wire,
bills go silking through the air,
they have no place in this existence.
It's her smell, her warmth,
her life to squander fatly wreathed
in smoke and dimpled fingers grasping just another cake
and no one else can say
her hair is dirty–
sniff around the crotch of stiffened pants
and arch an eyebrow at the mess she's in.
And we watch, helpless from the sidelines, frightened of the vortex,
scared to reach too far
because she's shown us
that the years of duty, order, form
are brittle as a carapace
will dust as easily as sun-bleached silk.

It's just as easy as letting go.

Losing battle, winning war,
The disappointment that keeps on giving.
The little things and every silver lining has a cloud.
While everyday leaves you a little less,
A weekend away with no sun.
Late nights, red lights and the need to need someone.

Back When I Started
By Eddie J Carter

Depression is a friendly face,
she takes her time with me,
lets me shuffle on.

She does not challenge like the others,
just lets me drift
to sleep in the day.

Depression is not mean to me,
by telling me everything I should be thankful for,
when all I want to see is black rot.

She lets me cry at the Christmas dinner table,
without fussing in embarrassment
and trying hard to carry on.

Depression allows my darkest thoughts,
sees them as valid options,
welcomes their release.

She stacks up the list for me,
tells me it's insurmountable,
better to shelter behind, in shadow.

Depression is my blanket,
a drag weight used in drowning,
a warmth from which there is no waking.

She throws her arm around my shoulder,
pins me down until action weeps from me,
creeps back in the morning to stop me rising.

Depression is a friendly face,
she takes her time with me,
lets me shuffle on.

Black Rot
By Andrew Barnes

Several unanswered calls sat
tiered in your smartphone, not so smart
now as they sit ignored on the leather arm
of the chair that your mother prefers.
You haul your weariness off the sofa, sway
like loose sails and sashay to the Zanussi
in the corner. Anxiety and tremors plunged
into gaping pockets of a cardigan,
bobbled by reluctance to wear an alternative.
The fridge white, proud with pupil shrinking light
chills the Smirnoff on barren shelves.
Only your mother's dinners take up a little space,
with their quilting of mould, a velvet hat on a mound of stew,
handed over with concern and the yard brush of
her mind, sweeping it away and under.

You brush your teeth slowly, methodically,
pushing the minute hand over into afternoon.
Perspiration beads on your hairline, you relinquish control
curl on the couch, drape your form with the beaded shawl.
Like sequined rain, the magic unfurls in your veins,
eyes glazing over, you slip, sliding away where it's
easier to be lonely, for a while.

Previously published in Voices from the Cave (May 2017 Revival Press) and in From
Doll House Windows.

Layering Time
By Lorraine Carey

Answerphones reluctantly
replied in flat voices
that didn't listen.

Pills waited in blister packs
on the top pantry shelf
while you rocked.

People would be coming in,
shaking bright umbrellas,
putting on kettles.

They would hear a silence
filled with fear
and a click.

Ending It
By Carole Bromley

Arrives quietly
on a Wednesday afternoon
gradually fills
up your doorway
until you know
you'll have to invite him
to stay.
Come in from the cold you'll say,
shake his hand,
open your heavy wood door
wide
offer him steak and fish;
Whiskey to keep him warm.
Here's my comfortable chair by the fire
you'll say
in your best welcoming voice,
here's my bed it's king-size,
there's shutters to keep out the noise.
You'll serve him breakfast
eggs benedict on your best plates.
Stay as long as you need,
you'll say.
Treat him well
and one day
soon
he'll leave
quietly,
the same way he arrived.

Mister Depression
By Catherine Whittaker

I was eight years old.
He smiled at me across the kitchen table,
showed me the scar on his side where he'd
aimed the gun and tried to "end it all."
He could only eat baby food,
offered me applesauce,
and we laughed about
his botched attempt
at escape.

Carl Ray's First Attempt
By Connie Ramsay Bott

I thought mine was the longer journey.
We'd spent a day and a half in the car.
You never left North Carolina.

Your dad's funeral was the week before.
The gossips were no doubt
just hitting their stride.

The first thing you said was,
I want out of here.
No doubt your mother felt the same.

We piled into two cars:
six kids, two dogs,
a couple and a half.

We drove till we got to the place
where the continent edged the ocean,
where the waves crashed and the land
held its ground, washed clean,

and the blue went on forever.

Small Town Suicide
By Connie Ramsay Bott

Paralytic in darkness,
this gnawing numbness
pours out all over
my sickening flesh.

Voices like explosions.
This deafening heap
of mechanical sounds
and foreign colours,
flows out all over
my suicidal mind.

This substanceless blue.
Shadows. Deadening.
Flashing. I start to percolate.
Regrets. Ruin.
This guilt.
I unpeel.
Something else.
An arc of brilliance,
I cannot catch.

Dead hands clench me.
Committed to the crime,
they melt me into the red.
I am not the kid in the pictures.
I am woefully insipid.

The Ills
By Earl J. Guernsey

A sick familiar, the shadow,
the one who walks beside you,
glimpsed in peripheral vision,
the other, there in the mirror
staring back at you.

A swift plunge,
the hangman's drop to Hades
where skeletal hands
reach out to pull you in,
Dante's stinking demons
crowding, chattering,
picking at your brain, teasing out
filaments, exposing nerve endings
with filthy fingernails, dripping venom,
scrabbling to uncover synapses of reason,
unravelling fronds of neurons,
a frenzied opening of a black stream
of self loathing.

From a Deep Enough Pit
By Sue Mackrell

And then the wasteland.

Stasis, a nihilism of despair,
white ice, numbing, in a creeping,
barren expanse of frozen tundra.

They say that from a deep enough pit
you can see the moon at midday,
and the dark phase is revealed
as the new moon rising in daylight,
its crescent reflected as a faint earth-shine,
ascending brightness transcending the shadow.

And you know that
this pall of black will pass
and streaks of sunlight
will diminish the dark.

Published online on the Survivors' Poetry website where it was Poem of the Month in September 2010.

In the ever falling debris,
of this changing and framing world,
a place where all possible futures
have already been sold,
he tries to breech
the tides of faceless people
who refuse to endorse
his separate existence.

At the shop that sells lifestyles,
he stops,
searching the windows of opportunity,
finds only the incremental tellings,
of an ancient animal altered.

He recoils,
at the grotesquely familiar
reflected.

As a ghost in his own life,
John resumes the search for symmetry;
seeking a truth
that needs no reflection.

It is at the waterhole, he finally learns
that he who fears his own reflection,
will eventually die of thirst.

Ghost
By Niall O'Connor

there is this trembling
inside this ribcage.

an earthquake of
being alive

and I am completely
terrified of ripping myself
apart.

Depression is a Gun
By Melissa Jennings

At edge of town I once saw Loneliness
sitting with his friend Together,
sleeping in a shelter.

I, heading home from nightshift to family,
was alone, not lonely.

But they were there together, huddled
for heat in the long cold night.
Each was all they had.

Soon, on some cold or stormy morning
one would fail to wake.
Then the loneliness would double,
being alone, utterly.

Loneliness
By Martin Swords

Been floating in the sea of life
blind to the dangers
of the water.

Until one day
a storm got too wild,
tempests raged, riling up the waves –
a tsunami over my head.

And I've been drowning ever since,
breathless under water,
but somehow
still alive.

Body starving for nourishment
a soul void of happiness,
I continue to linger,
mindlessly carried away
with the currents of the ocean.

One day I will be gone
or else washed up on a shore,
both scenarios better
than endlessly drowning in sorrow.

A Raging Storm
By Jeremy Mifsud

When we talked about self harm in lesson
You pulled your sleeves down to cover your wrists.
Everyone laughed about 'emos';
I sat in silence and wondered if they knew.

When we had lunch after a lesson about eating disorders
You didn't eat anything and went for a walk.
Nobody noticed you wasting away;
I sat in silence and wondered if they knew.

When they talked about suicide in the lesson,
You weren't in. Nor the day after or the day after,
Weeks went past. Months, then years;
I sat in silence and wondered if they knew.

Life is a Lesson to Those Who Listen.
By Andy Horwood

How it felt –
my life in the
palm of my hand,
hot with death
as I tried to kill it.

Look at it there –
this shrivelling,
shrieking wreckage
of a once great promise.

At least that was what I was once told –
that I held such enormous promise
and that, the world was within my grasp;
'You can be anything you desire, my dear;
Do you see it all?
The thousands of pictures
you could stitch yourself in to.'

How it felt –
to have the world run away
like so much water
between my fingers.

Look at it there –
the world,
my 'promise',
those thousands of pictures,
puddled and stagnant at my feet.

On The Pedestal
By Earl J. Guernsey

No time to think, no room for that.
Shostakovich, nearly tuneless, but beautiful to me
Screaming at my senses
Urging the mist to lift
So that I may see with clarity.
Nobody else knows the mist is there
I carry on as usual, the object of my love
Completely unaware.
My heart is bruised as the mist descends
No. 2 in E-Minor floods my soul
One bad experience and everything ends
I am crushed, while all around me think I am whole.

The Mist
By Barbara Derbyshire

Starved
I laid on my bed
fed but hungry,
taken care of
yet neglected
loving yet unloved,
and no one
could see past my
fake smiles;
I guess I could pretend
happiness well
glue myself together
in a way
that no one knew how deep the
arrows of my sadness laid
so that when I did weep they accused
me of lying—
I wish this pain were a lie
wish there was some way I could flush
away this agony
that hangs heavy on my bones,
and the insults of bullies that still ring in my ears
because I can't let it go
as I'm always told to,
I would give anything to be like autumn
shedding her leaves,
all I can pray for is a trip to the ocean
where she unfolds her waters
eroding away all my agony for a time.

Suitcase of Depression
By Linda M. Crate

Bury my face in the pillow,
Bury my tears in the down,
Bury my mouth in cotton sheets -
Bury escaping sound.

Bury my pain in anger,
Bury my fears in your touch.
Bury my hurt in denial
when it gets too much.

Bury the truth in fantasy,
Bury my head in the sand.
Bury my eyes in your soul,
Bury my life in your hands.

When the weight has lifted,
when my freedom has been found,
when relief has come to me,
bury me in the ground.

Buried
By Spreken

She sits quietly unspooling
in the sterile room.

Words sink
through unfamiliar openings,
letters unroll, drift

down her chin, slide
over breasts, the hip and thighs,
onto toenails and skin.

Broad vowels sit fat
on her tongue,
move like slugs
weary with their own shape.

Consonants slip out of bends,
there's a comma in her eye,
semi-colons in her ear,
a full-stop lodged
in her belly.

The closed bracket of her mouth
is a fault line opening
and closing.

White noise mushrooms inside her.
The day says nothing.

Word Search
By Eithne Lannon

At five thirty-nine am,
there is no one around to hear you,
nothing to dampen the abstracts
and give you concrete feet.

Let the rattle of the fridge
muffle out every last regret,
beget another emotion
snuffled out into the ether.

In the silence
you find a vision of yourself
with stretchered jaw and nee-naw teeth
demanding an ambulance.

The paramedics can't fit the oxygen mask
over your screaming. Anaesthetic needles
bend against your fits. The last rites are carried out
under a streetlamp that flickers as you grind.

They wait until you're finished.
The gurney waits there too.
No need to strap down a cadaver.
One more body bag to play Christmas with.

Then, inside the night air,
the breeze detects a tiny heartbeat
and the Empyrean comes to lift you along
into the fire.

There Must Be Ashes
By Colin Dardis

Don't touch me   I may shatter
you can speak to me
but don't touch me   I may shatter

you can look at me   even look through me
just don't get too close
shush, don't raise your voice   I may shatter

don't sit too close
try not to judge me   if you do
I may shatter

if the light shines at just the right   angle
you may see yourself reflected in   my face
please don't scream   I will shatter

and you will have to pick up the pieces.

The Glass Delusion
By Raine Geoghegan

Two

Love your brothers and sisters, Momma said
carry us like a song in your heart.

In high school, I whispered gossip to mean girls
and, on alternate Tuesdays, tried to not to drown

in labels
and expectations

and a labyrinth of dented lockers
that made hollow sounds

when bodies and metal collided
for the thousandth occasion

at the same high school
at the same time

my brother was molested

we didn't learn what happened 'til years later
after he stopped coming home.

On a field trip with an overnight bus ride
two rich boys—also brothers
pinned him in the corner of the high, stiff seat
used some sort of hard implement

one of them held a knife
it scraped the metal frame around the window
screeching metal around a black night
swallowing all those stars

anyway, that's what I heard
third-hand, from our mother
or fourth- or fifth-hand, if I am counting
the rich brothers.

The Sound of Metal
By Anna Kander

In English, there are at least nineteen words
to describe the sounds of metal:
clang, ding, clatter, clunk, clash
drum, echo, jangle, rattle, rasp
jingle, gong, plink, tinkle, crash
wood blocks make dull thumps

strike metal and it sings
releasing sounds sharp like weapons for avenging.

The energy of struck metal dissipates slowly
scientists say that's because metal is 'elastic'
I'd say metal remembers

the oscillations of metal decay—yet linger
my brother went silent; the metal still screams

every autumn, as purple and gold leaves fall
from the copper beech and sugar maples

my brothers and sisters who can travel
return to our hometown,

migrating back to the place of our birth, like salmon
until we are someone's dinner.

We will clink forks and knives on the good china
and enjoy a ritual meal

we had all our friends in common
and I'll see them around town
when I run to the drugstore for shampoo and chocolates
pieces of home that I forgot to bring

tokens of appreciation that somehow slip my mind
every single goddamn year

your friends from high school will ask me about you again
and I'll say no, he won't be coming home

no, he won't be here
for thanksgiving

First appeared in Degenerates: Voices for Peace

Loud red,
fire-engine red
alarm on his arm
screaming.

Emergency dispatch, please send one of each:
a cop, an ambulance, and a fire-truck.

We might need everyone.

Wet, smearing
blood, thin like water,
making doctors wonder.

'Fish oil supplements', he answers with pique.
'I'm trying to take care of my heart.'

This is not advice.
This is not a how-to.

This is the worst f**king misuse
of a deft hand and silence.

Cutting themselves is supposed to be
something only girls do.

The unsanitary secret: humans hurt themselves
when they're hurting and nobody's helping.

Siren
By Anna Kander

We break glass in case of emergencies
inflict harm so we can predict it
retake blasphemies
like
violence with words
or fists
or dicks.

We make pain part of us
build scar tissue around it

live past shards

The topic of this poem—
a taboo that keeps welling up

from children and adults
for whom we haven't made places
to feel safe

who still aren't
being

heard.

First appeared in Awakened Voices.

Midnight in the century at Oxford Road.
You meet me at the late-night Tesco there,
your eyes Medusa blank, demand I swear
to friends you're not fifteen but really old.
And if I don't, you'll kill yourself, explode
the myth I understand your pain, or care
about you. Terror grabs my throat, yet where
the lie should form, the tongue says 'please come home'.

You're thirty now. I still don't understand.
You didn't die but neither did the pain.
Back from Berlin and still without a man
you shout at me some stuff that sounds insane
and with my sharpest kitchen knife in hand
you say you want to kill yourself again.

Circular Time
By Ruth Aylett

Can good fruit ripen on a mawkish vine?
I doubt it.
But perhaps there is still time
To save my kids?
Pick them, quick!
Then stick them in the sun
Far away from me
So I'll not poison them with insecurity
And fear.
I'll stand over here,
In shade,
And watch their rosy goodness made
Complete,
In hearty heat,
Without anaemic chills that drain their strength
Depleting
Mighty spirits with which they came.

The Fruit of My Womb
By Carrie Danaher Hoyt

Oh Lord, let me feel human.
  Just for a second,
      a fraction,
          a moment.
To be over-flowing,
        re-born,
torn from the numbness
    inside of me.
Adorned with normality
and to know what
    alive feels like.
To open my eyes
and find the mist gone
and in its place
a sun-kissed dream
singing paragons of hope
    that allow me to
breathe in new shades,
instead of the greys
of my broken will.

Jane's Prayer
By F.A.Peeke

For those who keep
    their love near
to not view me as ill
and whisper pale voices
tinged with sadness and fear.
To walk with purpose
and know there is a
    reason for me;
that I am not surplus
because I can see joy
in the inanimate,
feel love as well as pain –
Oh Lord, how I long to feel
   human again.
Just for a second,
    a fraction,
      a moment,
  just to belong –
     just to be part of
the world's natural song.

Bed by midnight, I set my alarm for two a.m.
At its sound I pad to my son's room. The floor
is a rubble of clothes, guitar leads, a trophy cabinet
of sticky bowls residue in a corner.

In bed, he holds the glow of his screen,
perched in fear of the grave hymns that sing
in his dreams. He says he's okay, without shifting.
I fail by saying 'try to get some sleep'.

I retreat to my bed, risk an hour.
At three he's still glowing. Says he tried.
I know. Best rise for a time.

I wipe last night's words from the kitchen table.
We eat cereal to silence, see if that works.
It's being tested with everything else outside
the covers of a book. Back in bed,

he turns to the wall. Now I stay, see him to sleep.
At the inhale of day, the sun cracks its knuckles
behind the curtains. 'Come on then,' I say.

Night Watchman
By Peter Raynard

When my mother calls me "shy",
I simply look up, with fire blazing
in my eyes. I don't reprimand her.
But my words slather around
her like white cream on a cake.
"There's nothing wrong with being shy, is there?"
She stays silent, then. She probably wonders
why I don't say what I want to say and why
I keep my feelings concealed. I embed
the conversations I could have with
strangers inside me so deeply that every
unspoken dialogue wedges itself uncomfortably
onto my lips, trapped in a prison of my choice.
Sometimes, it's hard to emancipate compliments
or even, criticism. Sometimes I like smiling more than
plating my opinion and serving it to people waiting
for it. And, sometimes, I just shuffle my feet from side
to side nervously when someone invites me
to their home. There's nothing wrong
with being shy, I tell myself. I inject this
phrase into my bloodstream until it becomes a
part of who I am. If shyness were a disease,
hundreds of people like me would stay
boxed up in their houses and never come
out. If shyness were contagious, I'd
probably jump off a cliff and also
feel self-conscious while doing so.

Good Thing, Bad Thing.
By Avantika Singhal

I am very confused by the world.
It's like a Rubik cube
that I twist and turn;
I can never find the sequence.
I prefer to float in my bubble,
looking down on people and the
things they do.
I am not saying I am above them.
No!
I am saying I can't be among them
because they don't understand me.
I don't blame them.
I annoy them.
I copy them.
I antagonise them.
Ask me to explain why
and I feel like somebody swimming
underneath an iceberg.
I retreat into fantasy
And talk to my imaginary friend
And send myself text messages
And live in my head
I'm around the bend.
That's what you think, isn't it?
I am outside.
I never know what to say.
Nobody calls at the weekend.
Everyone stays away.
Sometimes I feel invisible
like I am
watching a film of myself.
Maybe one day I will become an actor
and take on a role so I can be somebody else.
I don't really want to be me.

Girl Outside
By Alan Savage

We are as one
my damaged girl and me,
drowning deep within her constant need
and my unrelenting sense of responsibility.

She has two thoughts, black and white
She has two emotions, love and hate
She has two judgements, goodness and evil
there is no middle ground
they call it borderline

and we live on the border of life,
like refugees in our own diminished detention centre
waiting indefinitely for good news, for normality, for acceptance

while we wait I learn the language
of our new world
but the words all sound the same
psychology psychotherapy, psychotic, psychosis

she waits desperately,
chronic intensity
raging raw against invisible walls,
cutting to cope, for a sense of hope
cutting to release, for a promise of peace
cutting to feel, cutting to heal
cutting to breathe, cutting to believe
cutting to survive, cutting to stay alive

Borderline
By Hilary Walker

abandonment - her worst fear,
the all too familiar mantra sounding loud and clear,
in my ear: I hate you, please don't leave me

I have more than two thoughts
I have a million, and then a million more,
they litter the floor, they hide behind the door,
they shout, they scream, they whisper, they roar

One more dance with the devil
One more midnight deal with god
One more last chance
One more...

They tell me I'm now a carer, but some days I don't care anymore

but we are as one
my damaged girl and me
for the scars that cover her body
bleed deep into my heart.

Sadness
and fear of the dark
pull me back
to a childhood memory
with the feeling
of helplessness.

The warmth
of your laughter
brings me back to the present.

Oh, I know,
you too
have your own fear,
your own sadness,
your own dark.

Fear of the Dark
By Galya Varna

Teach me to build a den down by the beck,
how to pond-dip water snails, sticklebacks;
teach me the kindling sticks to pick to build
a campfire, how to mount a stone surround
to keep me safe; teach me how to light it,
let it burn to embers before baking sour-
dough bread on willow sticks; teach me how
to live without the essentials: running water,

flushing toilet. You. Teach me how to forgive
a lover who doesn't deserve me, how
to raise a family alone. But don't teach me

how bleach can't clean everything.
Don't teach me how a bridge
over the M1 is the only way out.

Meg
By Rachel Davies

Each time I flick a light switch
I see Mother strapped to a chair.

A white-coated man throws a lever.
Her body thrashes like a live cable.

I nurse my heart with its image
of Mother framed in the doorway,

dressed as if in mourning,
her temples blackened

from repeated shocks.
I nurse my heart for the Mother

who never came back.
She lived in a darkness

no prescription could lift.
I am the soot from her chimney.

Soot
By Owen Gallagher

I have seen that bed before in your bedroom.
I have stolen from beside it.

In the piles of rubbish there were razors.
I took them, wrapped them in toilet paper,

so you wouldn't become blood brothers
with an unsuspecting bin man.

I threw them away - couldn't stand to leave them,
to make it so easy for you to break something I adored.

I have tidied that mess a hundred times.
Thrown away the bottles and tissues,

tidied up the piles of clothes – still tagged.
Folded them into drawers.

I find such comfort in order.
I tried to share my safety with you

but you are like a spinning top
only alive when the world is a blur.

That is not Tracy Emin's Bed. It is my Sister's.

By Genevieve Glynn

I cleaned away the dirt and opened the window –
to let some of the sadness out.

I knew a tidy room and fresh air was not enough,
but it made me feel a little better about leaving you alone.

We used to sleep in the same house, in the same room,
in the same bed. There was another room

and another bed but every night we'd fall asleep
accidentally on purpose - together.

You have bad weather in your rib cage
and my stomach is the bottom of a deep dark sea.

In each others company we could settle and sleep.
When you woke in the night you cried hot angry tears.

When I woke in the night I'd call your name
like an ancient prayer to keep the dark away.

I don't call any more. I am older
and you are far too far too far.

When she's high she's hello yes yes spraying pigments splashing off the wall and her hair twisting fizz and orange pop when she's low she leaches sucking light from all around and shadows fatten where she sits when she paints she's brooding brown her pinpoint eyes blur blue.

Colours
By Rachel McGladdery

Up the gravel drive we go, in our well-made car.
Neat lawns and hedges give away
To the house up in the distance
I can see sheets billowing
I can see a pond (would that be really there?)
Reflecting March's sky
Blue and yellow and higher than my mother.
We take our tea upon the lawn
Brought by a sweet young thing,
Crisp in her linen
And Doctor Green sucks on his pipe and tamps it with a thoughtful thumb
And tells us that she's 'quite, quite mad.'
We are content with this.
He puts the thing to bed, tobacco rolling round our ears in tweedy comfort
Brownwood, a decent fire
Books, leathered tooled - a spaniel at his feet.
Later we go and watch,
Her nightdress billows through the corridor
Her hands describe things eloquently and she sings a doctrine to whoever will stand long enough
She tells us that the doctors all are stupid,
They haven't even heard of Goethe
She's underwater now. The silver hypodermic took her there.
Our Ophelia, floating hair like knots in trees.

Bare white feet.

Ophelia
By Rachel McGladdery

That one snatch of lyric is you.
Unlike your namesake bird,
you didn't rise from the ashes
(and, yes, that was your real name.)

Our friendship one of bands, music,
stories and fanzines. I supplied
reviews, news, interviews and poems
you published alongside your stories
where reality slipped, became an itch
burning a bloodstream, a ghostly
cloud of ashes only you could see.

You thought it made you a burden,
as if friends were forced to shoulder
the weight of your rejection slips
when they only saw the acceptances.
Your parents wrote you off, told you
to snap out of it, stop being so moody.

The Gift of Sadness
By Emma Lee

At a quarter century, you vowed
you'd go no further. One hundred
and twenty miles away, I didn't know.
You died in my birthday month.
You missed my wedding, my daughter,
my husband's funeral, but I carried
you there voluntarily. I can't forget.

Your parents' words were a hollow
you'd retreat into until I could tug you out
with a ribbon of cassette tape,
wrap it into a vinyl spiral,
a stylus needle to stitch words
with music, wishing I could
get you to spiral out instead of in.

You didn't rise from the ashes,
unlike your namesake bird.
That one snatch of lyric is you.

(i.m. Phoenix, 1969 – 1994; Title is a quote from Rosetta Stone's "Subterfuge")

My clothes are a pile of ugly cocoons
they make me cry
remind me of childhood
everything stacked
on the edge
about to topple

Should I show the sink my face?
I smell incurable

With the steam
comes a kettle of anxiety
Has somebody pissed in here?
Where is my purse?
What did I say before I went to sleep?

The white slug on the toothbrush is me
balancing
only just

Today my only function will be
to leave lipstick marks on mugs.

Morning Sickness
By Michelle Diaz

It's 01.20 in the morning and you're awake
awake
awake
I offer you my breasts but you don't want them,
which makes me feel strange and redundant.
We struggle in each other's arms as you twist
and writhe, reel backwards, lead me in a stilted dance
across the carpet, the sea-green carpet, which
is also the ocean floor, bumping against the shipwreck
of your cot, dragging us under. The
bubble-wrap tentacles of an octopus wave
mournfully from the ceiling, clashing
against our iron weight.
Your gull cry pierces the night. You are
angry with me. You point at the door, "da da da",
as my milk chokes in your throat.
What more do I have to give you?
Not my heart, you already have it.
They ripped it out of my chest when you were born,
grafted it to your back with paste and a palette knife

Weaning
By Victoria Richards

while they stitched me back together.
It bleeds openly, that's why you sleep
on your front, even though you're not
supposed to, because of SIDS. In
the mornings your sheets are sodden red,
and so is your hair, my blonde, bloodied, darling boy.
You wouldn't like my tears – they
only fall in small, dark spaces, when
I read something sad on my phone
about lions or kids getting killed in America.
Take my mind – you're welcome to it, though
it is broken, so you might not enjoy it much.
I left it behind at an 18-course tasting menu at the
Dorchester, layers on layers on stark, white plates.
There was foam and something called a velouté
that we paid £180 for, so we pretended to love it,
called it "rich and complex", narrowed
our eyes and nodded. I'm not sure I even liked it,
it left a strange, sour taste in my mouth, but –
I don't know what else to feed you.

My knees are tough as nutshells,

skin in scrubbed mahogany spots,
brown like old pennies.

I kneel.

I seem to be always praying to the Gods of Shit and Hell.

Their muck is everywhere –
has got into the chinks in my brain.

I can smell it.

I whiffle the air, hound on the scent.

Who the fuck wore their shoes in the house?

Oil trailed smears from careless feet taunt me with their calculated
blemish.
Spots mark a circle, an occult trap through which I cannot pass.

I hate you.
I hate you.

Sad scrubber, burnishing marks.

Back curving with ache from the crouch.

Dogs, dreaming on sofa cushions, gently woofing in their sleep.
Their dander on the rug,

tenacious amongst the fibres.

I pluck at them, fingers swollen,

Diagnosis
By Jane Burn

pile them in cobweb pyramids, soft as butterflies.

Dirty as death.

My son, kicking out sweet baby legs –
his fat oaf of a mother crawling, hands and knees, walrusing the floor
in search of filth.

He smiles,

all blinky eyes,
gums bending round his baby-talk.

I kiss him, balancing on the balls of my hands.

I have boiled all the bottles, the knives I use to level spoons of
powder.

I am sorry for this my darling. My useless tits made nothing.

I am dry, but still I ache to put them in your mouth.

I got my pleasure today from mopping tiled floors.

The rain blurs the windows, does not tempt me out.

My insulation against the world feels insubstantial, like a crochet
wrap.

I vacuum my world into lines.

Make soup, make tea.
Write words.

Malt and calciumhydrogenphosphatedihydrate,
niacin,
hydroxypropylcellulose – warm, warm.
Bleeding in sweet, hot paths –
making its milked way to stiff guts.
Release a breath,
feel your heart,
pitpat,
pulse,
gnarl of stomach,
chew of bowel, seep, seep.
Shiver a little,
once in a while as if rime has crept behind you,
settled on your neck.
Sip, sip through the fleeting clasp
of cold – keep on seeing the little things.
See the chip on the cup where you put your mouth,
a fork with a fleck of gristle,
sitting the gap between the tines.
Sense the drowsy tow of night,
lay among the wrongness of pillows that form
strange valleys for your head.
Sink, sink –
become too conscious of bones beneath skin,
wonder if yours are as hollow as a bird,
wonder if you will ever make crow-flight.
The headlamps of passing cars sift through the window,
pleat the room in reflected light.
The world is a bauble of untold bits –
molecules of book, smile, toenail,
hat.

Horlicks and Sertraline
By Jane Burn

I build my days the same,
with atoms
of everydayness,
strings of tarmac, sunrise, chair.
Fancy your brain as a series of plates – the mattress is a seafloor,
shifting your silt.
A mourn of wind outside is the song of sand.
Your arms are growing numb, you are sapped –
the, gentle, gentle downstairs count of a clock is a comfort of
regularity.
Pull out the fingernail you have pressed, deep in the soft –
it has furrowed a crescent of bliss upon your palm.

I held you like this when you were a baby
close in to keep you still and calm,
close in to keep you safe and warm.

I dried your tears and smoothed your hair
and told you shush, don't worry Mummy's near.
Tried to keep out the worries of the world.

And I have held you close like this
so many times throughout the years,
to keep you safe and help you bounce back up.

This was my way of showing you are perfect:
when you failed a test or got a rotten grade,
when naughty boys got stars just for sitting still.

For every boy who called you dumb or dull,
and every girl who said that you were fat,
and every teacher who said ignore them and they'd stop.

For every job you went for but did not get,
the training schemes that led to nothing in the end,
the drink and dope and skunk that took you far from me.

Throughout the years, I held on and held tight,
you drifted further from me, out of sight,
until I saw your broken body, your final cry for help.

Today I hold you as we wait for the bed,
for now I know I cannot heal you with my love,
my hugs cannot put your troubled mind to rest.

Holding On
By Eithne Cullen

I cannot bear to see you cut with grief,
to lose your smiles and jokes and sense of fun,
the mischief and the sparkle of your eyes
that sometimes glaze with tears as you turn in
upon yourself and on your gaping sense of loss.

I am bereft as you are,
not for the loss of parents, but our friendship
which was built on solid ground:
on years of childhood, youth and adulthood-
births and marriages, milestones marked,
now rocky confusion takes its place... and I am scared.

Scared to lose you, as you come to terms with grief;
unable to endure your bitter casting off;
and as I try to hold you, calm your tears,
you cannot look me in the eye, but turn away,
I see that you will never let me help.
And I am the one left mourning for the friendship that is gone.

Bereft
By Eithne Cullen

This is a girl of seventeen, a side view,
seated on a swing
hung from a chestnut tree
her dress hitched by the wind.

This is a picture of my mother
before I was her daughter
before her father disowned her
before she married my father
before she had six children.

This was all before the swinging sixties
that could not free her
before the doctors
before the hospital stays grew longer
and longer,

before they fed the electricity
into her poor head that failed to help her
before the priest offered prayer as a cure
before the shock of her own mother's death
hit home.

This is my mother before I saw her
dead in the bed, her cold hands
clutching at air,
before life swung full circle
and could no longer hold her.

This is her on that green day
skirt askew, hair streaming out,
holding the ropes of the swing taut
rushing to meet her future
arcing in the air before her.

Previously Published in Lovely Legs, Salmon Poetry (Irl) 2009

Before
By Jean O'Brien

Three

I'll tell you this —
in hospital I'd turned into
a lioness, fought to get him
back from Special Care.
My tiny boy and I
came home.

I sank.
Back then the 'Baby Blues'
were cover for the hopeless days
the waking nights
the apathy, the dried-up milk
the guilt.
I travelled there.

And that's how I found myself
at pavement's edge considering
lorries, buses on that main road.
I was calm and never thought
of anybody else.

That day on Bridge Street
I was wearing my blue
raincoat so no-one saw
my baby boy
strapped to my chest.

I haven't spoken of that time
until today.

A version of this poem was published by The Interpreter's House, 2014.

On Bridge Street
By Hilary Robinson

It might've been better
if I hadn't began
braiding our three selves,
three scrap lives –
Mom and me and Brother in his crib.
But I was only five
and she sat, marooned, on the rug's blue gulf
having slid down the wall like a stain.
Maybe the when and how doesn't matter.

But Brother was in his crib and Mom cried
and cried. How could I not want to make it alright?

Braid
By Susan Millar DuMars

I am a puppet master,
I pull on my own strings and will myself
to move and speak
and breathe.
I am a mirror;
I reflect images of happiness
and fog up the ugliness of my truths.
The time came when I had to choose.
I willed myself to cut my strings
and to shatter my lies on the ground.
I am chaos.
I am nothing
but broken pieces who will myself
to move and speak
and breathe.

I am freedom.

I am
By Leila Tualla

1. *Can you tell me about yourself?*

Keep your self quiet. Keep it to yourself. Speak only of the automatic actions. Tell them of the shells. The ones that you gathered from every beach from Southend to Skegness. The bowl you keep them in. The gift shop you bought it in. Tell them that you keep them by the bathroom window, always open a crack.

2. *What interests you about this job?*

The Money is lurking in the corner of the room. Under the fluorescent light (flickering, natch) it's all tusks, and the animal smell of it sticks in your throat as you force out denials. Speak of anything but that rough grey skin, those flat feet made for trampling. The Money makes a sound between snort and cry as you squeeze out your feeble lie.

3. *What are your weaknesses?*

Don't tell them. Don't tell them about the thing you've always said was the worst thing you have ever done. Don't tell them that's a lie. Don't tell them. Don't tell them about the other thing you did. That you can't even bear to think. About the one that haunts you in your broken nights. Don't tell them. Don't tell them you can think of nothing else.

4. *Any questions?*

Bite your lip, consider carefully. Ask the square root of 72. Laugh at their surprise. Don't let the panic show in your eyes when they answer. You don't know what a square root is, and now you've been presented with a number. A trap. A number purporting to be the square root of 72, and no way to verify. Smile and laugh. Add this moment to the reel of stupid things that you once said to play on lonely days, or watch in the cracks of your broken nights.

Candidate
By Charley Reay (after Tara Bergin)

He called me damaged goods;
One of the un-dateable.
A worthy cause for charity,
But not someone you'd
Ever want as a girlfriend,
A live-in-lover, or a wife.
It hurt but he was right.
I traced the lonely line
Of my scar,
Sad that it would
Never be kissed.
The best thing seemed to
Be to turn from music
I could no longer dance to,
And stifle dreams
Before they woke.
Resigned and submissive
I spoke in a whisper.
Then out of darkness the others came.
They carried their imperfections
Unashamed; proud to be alive.
Holding the gift of measured days
In trembling hands as though
It was a flower, each petal counted.
They did far more than those
Who took their life for granted.
Their smiles were real; their joy was tangible.
And though they did not take away my fear
They showed me my beauty
My courage and my truth.
I saw the world anew with
Eyes that sparkled.
I left him there in the shadows,
And knew he'd got it wrong,
He was the damaged one
Made small with spite,
He wasn't worth the fight.

On the Shelf
By Jacqueline Pemberton

We've become so silent
because a lot of ears
are becoming closed.

We've become so silent
because we speak
and no one is comprehending.

We've become so silent
because our tears,
our pain and
our feelings
don't seem to 'top'
someone else's.

Becoming silent has
created a protection
from rejection and disappointment.
So I may look like I talk a lot
or write a lot,
but deep inside my voice is quiet;
Deep inside those raging thoughts
are eating me alive.

Stitches On My Lips
By Laura Ashley Laraque

my mother told me to be
wary of strangers,

so I became afraid
of the person staring back at me
in the mirror.

My Body is a Shapeshifter
By Melissa Jennings

Immobile, I lay waste to days
Letting dust gather at my toes
Pins prickle sat-on hands
I wait, resenting daylight

Purpose passes by the window
Stillness stares back
From a crumpled pile on the sofa
Blanket-soft, nose cold

Standing to swallow cheap comfort
I face down the silent wall
Fruit furs and collapses
I watch it drip through basket holes

This poem was previously published for World Mental Health Day at
https://worcestershirepoetlaureateninalewis.wordpress.com.

Waste
By Sallyanne Rock

Careless, a brush of the hand
is all it takes.
A glass, too close to the edge
smashes onto ceramic,
breaks.

The shatter, bell tinkle
brittle on the ear.
Shards glint, tears
frost the wash basin.

I scoop up the slivers,
grip them in my hand
they pierce my palms;
I cannot feel them.

All the pieces that are me,
shattered
sharp edged.
Broken.

Fragile
By Kathryn Metcalfe

This brain
was meant to be my offering
so I would not be thought a gate-crasher
at your garden party

               I tried
to save you some
wrapping it carefully in saran
held aloft with toothpicks to preserve
the topping   But I got hungry
along the way

               The years have gnawed
my impulse
control down to spotless
nubs (is this demyelination?)
I do not understand
these crumbs in my pocket
(are they poems?)

               Please forgive me
for arriving
empty-handed   I won't
stay long and I promise to sweep up
any eggshells from unintended
hatchlings on my watch

'Terra Incognita' was previously published in American Journal of Nursing, October 2014.

Terra Incognita
By Kim Goldberg

I see things, that aren't there
I cannot look at water
I see faces, and fire
I have, a repeat prescription
I am numbed by its effect
I think of death, a lot
I think of trains too
I like trains...too much!
I hear voices, they say bad things
I feel I should obey?
I think it shouldn't be, today
I attend the Desmond circle
I cry, and feel stupid
I am locked into my own psyche
I drink to much, and when drunk
I like to fight too much
I hate this weakness
I hate myself
I am a coward
I am losing
I am
I...

A Dangerous Year
By Adrian McRobb

Metal scrapes against bone
Twisting its way
Around my ribcage
Until I can no longer breathe

breathe

I claw at cables of steel
Barbs catch and rip my flesh
Coils tighten their grip
Suffocating, squeezing

breathe

This sculpture defines me
Forms me
Carves my mind
Weaving a new me

I can't breathe

Barbed Wire
By Emma Mooney

I call it
melancholy
because to call it anything else would
take away from all those people who did not make it out of
bed today, while I'm sitting here ready to go
nowhere

I call it
melancholy
because to give it another name would make a
mockery of those who are too numb to cry
too broken to be reached
too beaten to look for the light at the end of a tunnel they
never really believed in, because sometimes it is
all
tunnel

I call it
melancholy
because some days
the dark isn't even that dark
some days
it fills my pen with blood
and my veins with rage
and god knows I never did write better than when i was
suffering

melancholy
because any other word would be to forget all of those on
bridge edges
on window ledges
taking road trips in garages with the
doors closed

Melancholy
By Emma Page

melancholy
does not take baths with electric guitars
nor make toe rings of trigger guards
nor put everything on red
everything on red
everything
on
red

melancholy
did not hold a razor in my fist today
did not ram pills down my throat
jam escape up my nose
did not pack a bag of haphazard clothes
and run out on everybody who ever cared at all
not today
not
today

I call it
melancholy
because it sounds so much more romantic
so much more whimsical
so much less frightening for people who do not know what to do
with it
who hold it in their outstretched hands
the way men hold babies who are not theirs
terrified it will writhe and scream and demand to be quieted
comforted
made better
but there is nothing to make better
nothing to be made better

I am not broken;
some people are just
born sad.

I stand there and melt; I look like everyone else yet there's something different about me...I'm somehow broken inside but no one knows so they keep on misjudging me and treating me like some kind of an insect, an animal that has no voice.

I sit proud, I raise my voice to be heard among others, I manage to fly through interviews, that is until they see the real me, the broken me, the me that only me sees.

So as I get my tongue tied in conversations with management at work, tears begin to fall, I become red and feel the need to get away quick.

Yes, runaway, runaway, runaway.

Yet the faster I run the more they chase me, they chase me because they wonder whether I am worth the pennies that they supply me with each month. They are concerned so they mother cuddle me through giving me menial tasks to do.

Stigma of Mental Health
By Harriet Cooper

Just keep scanning.

Just keep scanning.
Supermarkets full of disgruntled customers who shuffle along with their trolleys looking for faults and trying to get the best deal.

For management, profit margins are key, they can't afford such like me.

There's no excuse for sighing.

There's no excuse for crying even when you feel like death inside.

You still have to smile.

Yes you still have to smile.

So I live in the hope that someday I'll cope and find a job that is rewarding and not so menial and boring.

Do not try to understand why
I stood on the tarmac, screaming for
jet engines to shut down
you have the keys, you open doors

I stood on the tarmac, screaming for
predicted moments, arrived where
you have the keys, you open minds
there is no place to hide

predicted moments arrive where
I scream, only to discover
there is no place to hide and
I will never hold the keys

I scream, only to discover
my mind locked, yet
I never held the keys and
jet engines still took flight

my mind unlocked
I kneel by windowed doors
jet engines still take flight
do not try to understand.

Admission Ward
By Carla Stein

Everyday, projecting an invention of myself,
talking too much, speaking too little,
wrapped in layers of self-defence,
needing to be understood, not knowing
what to say, always perched outside
the magic circle of belonging,

poised at the party's edge,
heart thumping, sweat crawling,
nausea pressing, world swimming,
longing to fit in, but reluctant to conform,
yearning for acceptance for
my unacceptable self,

this strange being, performing
amongst strangers.

Performance
By Sarah Evans

You're always smiling.
No darling, I'm always hiding.
And the cracks keep spreading.
Notice there are no eyes brightening
When the smile appears?
That's because it's fake, my dear.
You seem so happy.
Of course, it's easy.
Easier to paint a smile of lies
Than stumble over the truth
Because the truth hurts
And the truth bleeds
And the truth makes it hard to breathe
How can I explain that I miss a part of me
I never got to meet?
I seem so happy because I want to be
I wish I was a smiling queen
(Not suffering from PTSD)
Instead I'm a complete wreck
And yet,
I'm fine,
I'm fine, I'm fine
(Repeat it to believe it).
I've danced with these demons
For so long,
Fought to be strong,
Endured the rain.
Became a hurricane.
I may be always smiling
(Maybe to stop from crying)
Or maybe it's a grimace
(Wishing to endure less).

We Do What We Can To Survive
By D. E. Kerr

They were like banners,
proclaiming your induction.

They were like runes,
ancient, inscrutable.

They were like tombs,
commemorating loss.

They were like semaphore,
a frantic, unreadable signal.

They were like silences,
a grid of unspeakable hours.

They were like maps,
recording, imposing order.

They were like the I Ching,
each line and space important.

They were like cross stitch,
a habit for soothing your chaos.

They were like a journal,
your memories scoring the paper.

They were like souvenirs,
carried back from each visitation.

They were like a maze
I traveled to find your centre.

They were like a book
you sat and read to me.

Scars
By Kitty Coles

I sob
alone in skyscraper canyons
wait for the El, as snow layers.
I'm sub-zero frozen in two hats,
tartan scarf, fists snowballed tight
in sodden coat pockets. Santa jeers

from the brooch at my throat.
Frost diamond-locks my tears,
the plexiglass shelter brazens its lie.
I want to fall on the fire burning
beside the signals on the platform.
I want to be home.

But I'm here, another city, another country.
Another continent celebrates
a child born, loved, adored.
I sob alone.

Frozen
By Finola Scott

In the white room
a nurse holds my wrists,
dabs me with disinfectant-soaked cotton.
A kindly burning.

In the white room
I'm given a plastic cup
with a liquid that smells of blackberries
and tastes like soggy almonds.

In the white room
I'm allowed to dream
while two electrodes count the pulses in my brow,
two pens mark spikes on a chart.

And when I dream
the bed beneath me falls away
and I'm carried on cold fat rivers to the place
where the sea meets the sky;

and there I discover
I can unzip my human skin,
stretch into a world of seaweed and blue
with fingers made for swimming.

Selkie Games
By Andy Humphrey

They dance with me,
my sisters, among the reefs
where watching eyes will never spy us out.
We touch noses, kiss underwater;

our breath is bubbles
caught in a moonbeam's glimmer,
our heartbeats follow the rising and falling
of every wave, each tide.

The dreaming stops.
I zip up my skin, return
to the white room. The too-bright world,
garish, cold in its glare.

I let them prod,
knowing they will never
unstitch me, never drown the aftertaste
of wet peat in my mouth.

Four

You start at BBC One
as if sequential order is significant,
flick through a report on a war far away
then quickly switch to a documentary on Lunar Landings,
just as Mars comes into view.
Next a game show, a spin of a wheel,
a narrow choice of answer for the grand prize.
You wait to see them get it wrong,
say "Even I knew that!"
We catch the roar of a football crowd,
booing the decision of a referee, angry faces
peer close to the screen, we see a cop
interrogating a criminal, fists clench, the table shakes.
"You alright Son?"
Everything's fine I reply.
I want to say we are just watching television
But I don't believe that, I'm still seeing the war.
I'm trapped in the repetition of that square frame
where each click of the remote control
is a bullet in chamber, the tilt switch moving,
the trip wire starting it all off again.

Remote Control
By Glen Wilson

I am rushing home from work,
after only just arriving,
to check whether I turned the iron off.
As far as my colleagues know,
I'm meeting a client –
but not the one I saw yesterday
when I had to check the cooker.

Rushing
By Neil Elder

Listing countries of the world
in alphabetical order
has not helped Ellie to sleep.
Instead she is slipping again
towards the part of her mind
where thoughts run wild
like children on the last day of term.

When is final payment for the holiday due?
Her dad's cough – it's been too long,
the mole on her shoulder, it is getting bigger.
Should she change her password settings?
Did Tara really have to work late -
her voice seemed weird on the phone?
Ellie knows it's going to be hard in the morning
if sleep doesn't come soon –
But between pension contributions
and ISAs, she remembers tomorrow
is Friday, and pay day, all in one go;
sleep arrives to shut her worries away,
until tomorrow's big night out
when she'll have to decide what to wear.

Night Thoughts
By Neil Elder

When teaching Descartes, I dutifully described his dualism in detail.
I discussed his importance as the father of modernism,
But also his common ground with scholasticism.

Together we examined the ways he attempted to prove God
And the reliability of both mathematics and his own senses.
Also, some biographical information including his early education,
Military service, travels, and later work as a tutor to royal women.

I never told my students that, like Descartes,
It is easier for me to befriend women, but
I am still sometimes accused of being sexist or even
Typically male.

I didn't tell my students that, like Descartes,
I have at times been overwhelmed by grief
And felt ashamed while also becoming more patient with the
Grief of others.

I didn't tell my students that, like Descartes,
I tend to intellectualize and rationalize my problems,
Calming my anxiety with anything at all that I can know
Is certainly true.

What I Never Told My Students About Descartes
By Randall Horton

I don't think I mentioned in class that, like Descartes,
I sometimes wake to wonder where and who I am
And whether anything at all in the universe is not
Hostile to my being.

I'm sure I never brought up the fact that, like Descartes,
I sometimes scream out in my sleep, convinced that the
Evil demons pursuing me in my dreams are more real than
A perfect God.

And I certainly never told my students that, like Descartes,
I fear dying alone on a cold street in the wee hours of the
Morning, running from my personal problems and hoping
To find salvation.

On a scale of one   to   ten,
how are you feeling?
If ten is the best you have ever felt and one is the worst.
I am two five one six eight ten four three seven nine.
Every day I am all of these numbers.
Ask me what hue I am,
if purple is to happiness
what green is to grief,
as pink is to pain.
Ask me how I taste.
Bread and butter?
Mushroom soup?
You might as well ask in colour and food as numbers.

If Purple is to Happiness
By Jane Burn

I steal things.
Little, worthless things, not credit cards or handbags.
A very old book
because it smelled of age and made reference to bats.
A vase in a derelict house with a fallen roof.
I just have to have them.
I don't know why.
I guess I getf   i   x   a   t   e   d   on stuff.
My ornaments.
How they fill me with steady thrill,
how when I see
something in a junk shop,
on a shelf/table/car bootI pause   for a few moments,
enjoythe feeling I get when I see something I want.
Savour it.
Move forward slowly,
take the treasure in my hand,
feel the *beatbeatbeat beat beat beat beat beat beat beat*of
my heart steady out.
They comfort me.
The nights when I feel I have got this shifting in my head.
What does that mean?
Just that there are these plates in my head and some nightsmy brain
shifts in two,
goes hyperspace,
pan dimensional,tectonic, double screen.
S s P p L l I i T t T t I i N n G g.
Does it hurt?
No. But it I am frightened.
Likemy mind is a slide rule and I don't know why.

My axis is a blister pack
containing copper dots –
take one tablet three times daily
to subdue that feeling skin of yours.
Without it, I become
a wailing organ in a monsoon,
the eyeless monarch on the heath;
a roomful of smashed mirrors,
or a carpet of teeth, canine,
sharp and starving.
My axis is a blister pack
containing points of reference –
full stops that say there, now
pause and breathe –

see: a fat moon, a torch,
chamomile to taste;
plumes of smoke, burning peat
in the crisp air of October –
a coming sleep,
the quiet feather fall of dusk
and everything dressed softly
in its sepia self,
including me.

Points Of Reference
By Seanín Hughes

Dyslexic I am not
But I paddle the same cnut
Through the same waters
As some of you
Some shit went down
When I popped out
I bounced, Ma said
I took a clout,
Or something like that,
Something to do with my unformed head
She would always change the subject
So up I grow
Undiagnosed
Undisclosed
I walked on tiptoe
As though that's the way
That everybody goes,
I was a playground sensation,
I was copied by
All the other kids.
If we'd had Facebook it would o' been the nation
Some kind of tribute
Obviously
At least that's what I thought 'til the first boot
Sought to fill
My skinny arse
Followed by the cry of
"We've seen ya ballerina"
So much for being

DYSLEXIC I AM NOT
By Barry Fentiman Hall

Pied Piper of fashion
I was a rat
A brat
A spacca
An anagram
And a rum 'un.
I could not stay within
          The lines
Still can't sometimes,
A writer who cannot write, what's this?
A piece of genuine irony
Alanis?
Don't you think?
But through ten years
Of pointless Physiotherapy,
An aborted operation
And an affected strut
I managed to cover up
The things that cut
'Till the convulsions
Of my growth spurt pulled my head
This way and that
'Till my neck hurt more than after
I saw Anthrax at Bradford that time
In mosh pits
No-one can see you spaz
And they don't give a shit.
Mishapes, mistakes
Backwards heroes

Efulnikufesin
Is what it makes
And it was too,
In the sweat and the beer
I was tolerated among the stoners
Nothing to fear
From the damaged cases
I was unaware that I was literally a human jerk
Until I heard a guy at work
Remark how sad it was
Ma was still saying nothing
So on I spazzed,
Undiagnosed,
Undisclosed
Not yet Bazzed,
Somehow dating
And self medicating
Through years of unemployability and assessments.
Gone through the gears,
Learned to read
Upside down
And so a health scare got me freed
Made me aware
In Dr Walker's surgery
Of my ataxia
Those things that attack ya when you're trying to be cool
I had always been Cerebral
Now I was Palsied too
A defining moment

I was diagnosed
And the Doc and my Ma *ummed and aaahd*
And for a while you might say that I was scarred
But it is good to know, you know?
And after a while I begun to embrace the D, The D?
You know
The killer Ds
You and me,
The diagnosed
We may disclose or not,
As we please
We are
Dyslexic, Dyspraxic, Dysgraphic, Acrobatic; Disabled? Naah.
But an injury to one is an injury to all
If you fall,
I fall
We are Delicious, Desirable, Conspicuous, Bibulous, Joyously
ridiculous, Unbelievable, Indescribable, Undecipherable
And other words that end in able...
I am diagnosed
I have disclosed
And if the world cannot deal
With how I identify
My D fined rickety bits
Then you can kiss my ass
Not kick it.

Dyslexic I Am Not has previously been published at I Am Not A Silent Poet

In this renaissance,
this time of perpetual chaos,
as the current ripples through us,
we shut down our sixth sense and refuse,
self denial, anything right now would do,
anything to light up this fuse,
ignite a desire to move,
Winning streak fell short, turns out there is a thousand ways to lose,
running the rat race but the only way out is through,
though it is not always such a cruise
to live outside of this loop,
contra to all of their half truths,
propagated by those with set views,
but we decide what we defend,
our will they cannot circumvent,
the dark ones are very real,
no longer a concept so surreal,
on a subtle level it's something you just feel,
we cannot deny,

The Current
By Faatima Saleem

that they want us to comply,
but we are not undead,
oh the things they never said,
kept hush and thus we were misled,
time we let the old systems rust,
as led transforms to gold,
and the copper is no longer sold,
let it be known that we now have something more
within us there is much left to still explore,
from the lows of this plane we will once again soar,
nothing can stop the change,
it is too late,
we will not just sit and wait,
sitting ducks, enslaved,
for that thing upon which we often debate,
that concept called fate,
we have perceptions to bend,
ears to lend,
turns out it was just the beginning and not the end.

The anxiety
keeps me awake at night,
monsters I know are false
seem true
no matter how many times
I tell my mind to stop it insists
on going
down these roads,
and I've always felt everything so
deeply and profoundly
even when I feel nothing it feels like
a knife in my soul;
want to defeat this curse so I can finally
be free
find a way to breathe,
be able to sleep like everyone else
not walk on the needles
of all my worries,
nettling and biting until eventually my
body shuts off my brain
so I can get some sort of relief
I never remember when I finally fell asleep
sometimes I wake so tired I must sleep again
I wish I could just shake these neurotic
worries and stop my mind from wandering
in circles until it makes me panic.

Wish I Could Shake This
By Linda M. Crate

He choose deafness:
to smile instead at noise
that did not comprehend
his chambers hollow echo.

Deafness: to colour,
texture. Deafness
to pleasure:
that he took, at eight o'clock,
without milk and two sugars.

Deafness to sound turned
to songs of bullets.
To words of the hearing;
calling him simple.

Uniform: pinstripe grey,
burgundy tie, shoes
beyond a shine;
but polished anyway.

for appearances sake;
he chose deafness:
noise; barbed wire fenced
against screaming

while others fell:
brothers and sisters, blood
and words made flesh.
And bones. Deaf, immune to
their staccato sound.

Michael
By Dave Kavanagh

Doctor my heart is broken you see
Have you anything that will numb all the feelings in me?

It's my throat that is hoarse and shouting to be heard
I can't hold it in and not say a word

Can you stop all the thoughts and prescribe a pill
There's a migraine brewing and it is making me ill

My eyes are wide open breathing shallow not deep
There's overwhelming stimuli and I can't fall asleep

The food is processed and I can't break it down
The chemicals are killing me
Anything natural around?

I'm destroying my body and inevitably my mind
It's ironic that in fact we're know as mankind

I am preoccupied with symptoms
A hypochondriac you say
Despite the doctor's reassurance
I'm the victim in my play.

Hypochondriac
By Nancy Dawn

I want to go home
rocking child inside,
orphan – adult
the umbilical cord is

                                            cut

I'm free
(let me go back inside).

The Womb
By Isabelle Kenyon

Then I failed myself,
took out the heart,
watched the TV,
sang all the blue songs,
soaked up the whiskey,
the gin, the beer,
sweated blood
on high days and holidays,
stared at the sun
cried at the moon,
the poor souls that twisted,
the mean drunks that cursed,
and me, king of the lepers,
licking the sores of my mind.

Everything Failed Me
By Peadar O'Donoghue

Why has this river cut me into an oxbow lake?

Help yourself to some tissues.

Why has the past grown talons?

The present should have a greater wingspan.

Why can't I stop my sternum crumbling?

Make your exhalations longer than your inhalations.

Why am I a fat bramble: warped, ugly, hostile?

I just counted judgements as if they were beans.

Why has it been raining for nine days solid?

Depressions tend to come inland from the coast.

Why is the sky split across the middle?

I understand very little else about weather.

Why do you hate me?

Let's play catch with these stones.

Why won't God ever show Herself?

I have been telling you for an hour: I don't know.

My 9:45 Has Borderline Personality Disorder

By Olivia Tuck

That whatever you are, you need to destroy it.

That going for your cookie-dough skin with a razor stings
more than acting against it with fiercer tools, but
it doesn't matter: abandonment is what truly cuts.

That driving a dear weather-beaten psychiatrist
to earlier-than-planned retirement is easier than it sounds.

That you might see a rainbow when you wake up
at dusk; wonder if God won't flood the Earth again. Of course,
by three a.m. you could be up to your neck in ocean; playing
Charybdis, hauling angry sailors down with you.

That when you end up in casualty of a Saturday night,
nobody will materialise with cards or Tesco carnations.
(However, if you're a tad more experienced, at least
you'll have learnt where to find a phone signal,
about the range of gourmet packed sandwiches on offer,
which nurse will smooth your hair, and which will scrawl
across your chart in biro blood: *Manipulative.*)

That other People Like You are the only sweet friends who know
how to defend the jagged splinters of a child-
woman. We are the covalent bonds in a fucked-up diamond:
dazzlingly inseparable as we carry on falling.

Things Only Borderlines Know
By Olivia Tuck

That you can love others without loving yourself.
That you want to be loved as much as you can feel.

Solar flares. Wild nights. Broken bottles. Hailstorms. Hollow,
chocolate girl for Easter; eyes dead, smile warped.

It burns to come close enough to breathe
your smoke. That as much as you can feel is too much
to ask, but perhaps you could settle for the love of anyone
who would tattoo their initials over Ribena-dark scars, feed you
Turkish Delight promises, with steadfastness that echoes
through space and leaves marks that heal, and do not
ruin. A moon you can keep on a string round your wrist,
to linger. Although...face it. You are the satellite.

That shadows gain weight when you are alone. No power
supply. You reach out to touch what it means to be ash.
That if you try to leave, they've got thread. Water. Charcoal.
When you hear your screams, you want to disappear,
yet you keep this secret safe. In case you change your mind.

After the mental ward was smashed to rubble
the workmen doffed their helmets, cracked jokes,
mimicked the loonies' laughter and pulled daft faces.
But the rain forgave, forgave, cleansing shattered bricks,
slivers of glass, those cracked tiles where the crazies
wept, or all night stamped out a manic dance
or shuffled back and forth in a suicidal waltz.

For the out of mind dumped out of sight,
the tomb people who stank in their grave clothes,
no one raises a statue that screams their names,
or a shiny new plaque. These are the thrice - erased.
Yet when the workmen leave: wraiths, whispers.
Someone prays forever for peace that never came.

First published in Lagan Online.

Demolition
By Peter Adair

Two weeks ago Saturday last I had my first encounter with the
pigeon people.
Lying in bed in an empty flat I heard the first tell - tale peck.
Curtains drawn,
My tormenters were hidden from me
But my brain helpfully filled in the gaps of what I could not see.
Pigeon people at the window.
I'm trapped in bed, an ocean sloshing around my head,
A desert forming on my tongue,
A forest sprouting from my forearms,
And there are pigeon people at the window.
Perfect fucking timing.

It's my third day here.
But the first with the pigeon people,
So let's call it Day Two.
I hear compromise is very important in these situations,
So let's meet in the middle. Day Two.
That first peck has become a steady hammering
Coupled with the scratching of the woodwork any crumbs of doubt
that I had
That perhaps there was not actually pigeon people at the window
Have swiftly been brushed away.
There are pigeon people at the window
And I'm trapped in bed.
My ankles turned to lead,
My spine becomes another bed spring,
As the waves keep crashing.

Pigeon People
By Molly Frawley

Pigeon people have beaks.
How else would they peck?
But I'm not sure they have wings.
Maybe just really strong feathered arms,
Opposable thumbs,
Dark, soulless eyes,
And kind hearts.
Despite my unflattering description,
Looks can be deceiving and
The only villain in this story is me,
'Cause see, before the pigeon people arrived
That window was beginning to seem like my only way out.
'Cause I've come to feel more like a pane of glass than
Anything else
And three floors up I can feel the pressure building all around me.
With each new crack
I see the panic in my loved ones' eyes,
When I shatter how many shards will find their way to them?
Slice new homes for themselves in the hearts where I used to live?
But now there are pigeon people at the window.
So I'm trapped in bed.
Thank fuck for that.

Between green walls, these girls with glass skeletons
pitch and spill, tilt corridor to corridor
hiking off the last inches of skin. Like selkies
they want to exchange a life, step out of themselves into
a world of rinsed air –

Here the windows have catches. They are always closed.
Here there are no accessible stairs.

Faces pinched and sly as foxes, these girls are queens of lies
who step to court in paper robes and slippers, mobilised
by the need to touch with tender hands the bodies
of their weeping counterparts, to scan
for better bones than theirs with sweeping palms. Their hands
jump and stutter. They make sweet sounds they do not mean
and pat the knives of thinner shoulders.

The days leak and bleed like watercolours.
The sun burns, the mad moon makes her light,
but here, time is borderless.
The girls move grimly from meal to meal.
The knobs of their wrists gleam along the banisters.

Eating Disorder Ward
By Cheryl Pearson

All day their throats are stuffed with love, and facts, and sandwiches.
All night they move, exhausted,
revolving like the restless dead in neat, white boxes
of starched sheet and strictly necessary light.

Only first thing are they still. Frozen in their fierce,
geometric shapes, they hang on the scales,
white knuckled on the bars. Thin wrists starred with errors.

If they don't move, it won't happen.
If they are absent, it doesn't count.

At noon, their parents come. They've had to learn
the language. They still think, but no longer say,
You are worth your weight in gold.
They talk of plain days. Leisure. They do not talk of food.

The whole hour, they imagine trades:
their children for fistfuls of feathers.

The exhibition at the gallery is called
'Things you don't want to see'.
The entry is free so I put on a smile
and walk out of my life and into everyone else's.

In the corner my best friend is
crying behind a barrier that says
'do not touch the artwork'
and I try to get close but
the guard pulls me away and whispers, 'no'.

On the floor are all the things we want people to think we like
when really we just want to like what we see
when we look in the mirror
on the wall of the gallery
underneath a sign that reads
'is this really who you want to be?'

I enter the next room holding the programme
over my eyes to hide what I don't know is in front of me:
I've entered the room called 'news feed'.

Everyone is talking all at once,
and I dare to peek and notice
the walls are bleeding with their words
and that none of them tell the truth.

There's shouting, ranting, complaints
and declarations of love,
there's look at me, look at us
look at where we are and where you're not.

There's a messy pile of books
each page full of faces
I haven't seen in ages.

Blue Square with White 'F' in the Middle
By Jade Moore

Over there is a guy
pacing up and down not knowing
whether he's coming or going.

I look at him too long,
then I blink and suddenly he's gone,
and who knows when he'll be back?

My sister stands in the centre of the room
surrounded by a circle of friends
and her husband who all listen
to her opinions which are too loud for me.

So loud I need to put on one pair of the many headphones
that line the edges of the room, each one sitting suspiciously quiet
underneath a placard that says:
'The things you think you need to hear'.

There's a button with the whole world on its face
and I click it and wonder if I've stopped the human race.

I'm blocking out the voices of people I barely know,
and hoping that when I press the button
with the speech bubble my green light will come on
and I'll hear 'pah-king' and hope it's you asking
if I'm okay or what am I up to or do I want to get coffee.

And when it is, I drop everything
and log out of this exhibition
which I'm told is here 'for the forseeable'.

And I walk outside
to this place called 'real life'
and behind are my friends and family
following me, ready to escape,
ready to create and curate
their own gallery

which could be as simple as
one photo,
one feeling,
one moment...

You don't have to like it,
you don't have to share

the only thing that matters
is that you were there.

Concept: (n): an abstract idea; a general notion

Example: You rise from the smoke, skin dark with soot, as the sun stretches and yawns above the horizon.

Example: You chase that great star over war torn land, beating scars into the earth with your boots. Head held high. Wind at your back, ushering you home.

Example: Battle-weary, worn, you pull the sword from your back and rest at it at the door. Breathe a sigh. Embrace the dawn as it grows to day. A sight you've fought to see.

Example: The Gods crawl from the heavens, follow the trail of the tracks of your boots, whisper stories of your greatness and arrive at your door with songs in their hearts, on their tongues.

Example: The Gods bow to you.

Concept
By Lexi Vranick

I look at her,
how her hair falls to her waist,
how her skin radiates,
how her lips swell,
a full bloom:

First impressions.

I blink and stare again
at her hair breaking,
a mask for her sad eyes,
at her skin's purpled bruises: tainted;
her swollen lips

(She's dreaming of the day when happiness will greet her like a warm
embrace, but the corners of her lips are turned down.)

First Impressions
By Jeel Chung and Isabelle Kenyon

Ok. I read the label.
For the first week I keep the load light:
a slim volume of poetry,
two pens (with lids on)
an A6 notebook.

By the end of the month
I can't remember the capacity,
think I can fit in another book,
a mini first-aid kit,
some flyers, Sellotape and Blutac.

Then, the lids fall from the pens,
they leak on the notebook.
I throw it away and replace
it with a hardback one twice the size,
alongside three novels I am halfway through.

Add toys I am handed to "look after",
three conkers, a chewed lolly,
(that finds a corner so I can forget about it)
and sweet chestnut cases, that spike me
until I remember not to open that pocket.

I hear the bag strain and creak,
the lining rips
I keep losing things behind it.
The zip is broken half way
and still I load it further.

I stand on the tram platform
clutching a bag with a snapped strap,
surprised stitching has unravelled
the leather has worn through.
It couldn't take what I expected it to hold.

Warning: DO NOT EXCEED!
By Sarah L. Dixon

Five

Words in response to these by David Cameron, as food bank use tops a million this year.

'We've rescued our economy
Created record numbers of jobs
Put Britain back on her feet.
We've put our country on solid ground.'

And Mandy uses a food bank.
She didn't want to cos she's got pride,
But she's also got kids and a husband who's 'sad',
and pride doesn't fill empty bellies
even if it does nourish your soul.
And sometimes she's so hungry she can't concentrate,
or her hands will tremble as she lies awake,
Because the ground beneath her feet doesn't feel solid anymore.

So Mandy uses a food bank,
but she doesn't tell her mum.
Cos her mum's old enough to remember 1944,
How it was before.
And she doesn't want her to worry about this situation that she's found herself in,
this grim hanging on,
holding on, just fed by the kindness of a few.
When the ground beneath her feet doesn't feel solid anymore.

The Ground Beneath Her Feet
By Alison Down

And Mandy uses a food bank
with a voucher prescribed by her doctor to be redeemed for
emergencies.
But she can't even begin to imagine how she got here,
how she fell through a crack
in a system that's been broken by those well off enough to
Just Not Care.

And now here she is cupboards bare -
looking at long life milk and tinned produce from Poland and... and...
the ground beneath her feet doesn't feel solid anymore.

And Mandy works a job that pays the minimum wage,
And some days she don't see her kids till bedtime,
And when she rests her feet her ankles swell,
And she can't remember falling but she knows that she's been felled.

And her stomach churns for something better her heart yearns for
something better,
her head knows there's something better...
But the ground beneath her feet doesn't feel solid anymore.
Doesn't feel solid anymore.

In the cold light of the morning,
she wades slowly through the closed sea of irises.
Across the road in the Australian theme bar
Mr. Beagrie drinks his third pint of the day
watching News 24.

Mr. Beagrie sits alone
staring into his liquid gold.
She is there on the big screen, the Lone Ranger
of the Chelsea Flower Show,
hairdryers cocked at the ready,
coaxing the unwilling flowers
with warm electrifying air.
Mr. Beagrie doesn't give a shit
about flowers but he watches
anyway, as the irises unfold
startling white in the dawn
and his despair fills him
to the depths of his inebriated soul.

Mr Beagrie
By Rachel Burns

My country is 'bewitched'
My native people cannot come to terms
With how best to define how it feels,
You see, she has been complaining
of exhaustion of the heart and thinking too much,
My native people prefer not to interrogate
this as 'depression', they say it's impossible
This is just another white man's disease:
Omphile, South Africa's daughter suffocates!

So
My country is suffering from 'witchcraft'
Nigeria's son Yoruba cries of "Kpaja Kpaja"
(A bit of heaviness in the head
And pins and needles in the hands and feet),
Yet still they would rather claim it is Typhoid
Or Malaria, you see depression is the
Least of their vocabularies,
This is just another white man's disease
Only meant for the weaklings, (even
I did thought so at one point!)

But is it really? See the ball game just changed,
WHO crowned us position 21
In the saddest list of countries in the world,
It's been a longtime coming
But happiness finally kissed us goodbye,
And 'depression' well it just became
A black man's new ally!
Courtesy our own stereotyping
that had many silenced,
My country is now in pain
Wallowing in hate and bloodshed!

MIND MY MIND
By Spontaneous, The Poet

My country is sinking!
It has been doing that for days now,
When it simply cannot catch some sleep
'Cause a villain ordered a shoot to kill
Plan of action!
And by stray bullets its children are
Quickening to their grave,
Some are pacing towards it
making jokes out of the situation:
A stray bullet just passed!
A breadwinner tumbling down
Poverty just got redeemed,
Another just followed!

My country is drowning!
Its interests are slowly deviating
The international communities
are slowly pulling out,
She's loosing friends,
She's loosing that support system,
She's wallowing in her scars,
She's losing her grip,
Laughter, Assumptions, Rejections, Battles
She's slowly fading away
Always filled with anxiety,
"Forgive me" "Forgive me" "Please forgive me"
Guilt got her married to her own fears
She's fading, pacing, fading, panting, fad...

We need to help her
NO! we need shower her with all the love,
Accompany her for the therapeutic sessions
Interesting days at the gym, some jogging
Might help keep the heat up!
Just this once,
shall we forget our differences
And be her children,
Forget our political affiliations
And shun violent extremism
This is our disease,
Let's own up and fight against it!

Some people start their lives here,
others start here,
and some people start here.

Mark is late for school.
No clean trousers. Tie invisible.
Top button as open as a criticism.

His teacher admires his opportunism
but has heard all lies, yarns, and fairy-tales,
knows all excuses and elaborate details
used to pull the wool and veil
over the school's eyes.

Twenty years teaching multiplied
by twenty cigarettes a day =

History's his speciality. The maths isn't important.

Every other kid is able to get out of bed.
Every other kid is able to catch the bus.
Every other kid can do their homework
with negligible controversy or fuss

but Mark shirks authority,
drifts into fantasy during class.
Aye. This little shit needs a kick up the arse,
a measure of realism
poured in a glass.

Go home and dress yourself properly
then report immediately to my office –

Mark
By Stephen Watt

but Mark doesn't have the cash nor bus pass.

Mark's teacher drives him home.
Feels tarmac crumble
beneath expensive alloys,
a concrete jungle where disgruntled cowboys
huddle beneath tatty newsagent canopies,
weary of strange vehicles in their scheme.

A battered front door creaks open
where an elderly lady in a wheelchair
rolls into view.

Mark's teacher never knew that the boy was a carer
for his parent; an absent father
who daren't show face after his abusive nature
forced a mother
to take action, cut ties
and seek protection on the outskirts
where no one can hurt them.

Mark's teacher can now see the cuts
beneath his shirt cuffs, a clot of claret
like Mars winking on the clearest of nights.

On the gallows of a door handle,
the noose of a school tie
dangles like a warning
that an attitude has to change
and someone has to listen.

Some people start their lives here,
            others start here,
                        and some people are just trying to start,
                        anywhere.

And always the silent smell
Of music follows
Each time his name is mentioned
Never justice,
Covered in ignored pleadings
With pinpointed accuracy
Constantly kicking
The ladder away
From his freedom
Evidence suppressed and misplaced
For 16 years
In cross currents
Of ignored medical reports
Miscarrying justice
And innocence
Constantly brushed
Under the carpets
Drawn back on curtains
Across hospitals
And your bedroom upon release
Which eventually killed you
A terrible crime
With two victims.

Previously published on I am not a Silent Poet.

For Stefan Kiszko
By Andy N

On the back of his last can
and a bed sheet made of concrete
crumpled like an unwanted note
stolen from good intentions.
He lies on a disused public toilet floor
huddled against the door to keep the ghosts out.

His eyes set like salt water in open wounds
legs bent and feet hidden crowded by the urinals
he calls his Angels.
Who with outstretched porcelain wings
ingloriously stand over him.

Bedded down in the darkness
he fights with shadows
while match stick men play hang man
on anorexic walls.
And in between the spaces unseen
he counts his lost days on a calender
of broken dreams.

Chain Letter
By Anna Matyjiw

They are human beings
communication should be person-centred,
supportive.
Place the individual, their needs and aspirations
at the centre of care.
Uphold dignity.

Let us adopt an approach of recovery
enable people to sustain their personal identity.
Let us tackle discrimination,
preserve choice.

Talk about their life story,
provide a relaxed and secure atmosphere.

We are human beings
we understand and speak the same language
our needs are the same as yours.

We are not concerned with dignity
so much as being able to get up in the morning.
Recovery is not a word we understand,
despite speaking the same language.

Human
By Nina Lewis

Recovery
is a too far away dream,
one we no longer grapple with.

Today
is our recovery word,
just this day, just this one and then the next.
Listen to our life story when we begin
to utter and share.

In the beginning
there is only darkness.

Later, there will be light,
we are preserved until then, on medication
and the hope others have
for our recovery.

Six

Even the muse was suffocated
Beneath a mound of mire
Even the muse could not withstand
A constant line of fire.

The Carer Poet
By Margaret O'Driscoll

Where did you hide
arbitrary beast
fierce beast,
you will not bend my hand,
you will not take out my clothes,
I am edited differently, my grammar,
I've put all my eggs into riddles and sonnets:
I have a rope,
it's stronger than you think
I jumped roofs of three houses.
I have written squatting on the edge
of the wing of an airplane
I hung on a shoe
of the moon to love
I have sailed seas
to rescue seagulls adrift
I have tattooed maps for children play with me
I have lost them, I have returned them
to the breast of their mothers.
Here I am
a trail of crumbs waiting
to descend into God
knows where. I'm not going
to count steps.

Alzheimer's Disease
By Eduardo Escalante

'Do I know you dear?'
The question she asks
me every morning
with her lemon smile
and tepid eyes.

'I'm Denise, your daughter,
I say to the empty space
between us.

I wish she'd had a sudden death and
not this sleeping sickness
that makes a drought
of memory.

I show her photographs:
My first birthday,
First day at school,
Graduation,
The wedding.

Remember Me
By Jacqueline Pemberton

I want to plant a seed
within her frozen womb,
Let her recall that first flicker,
How she touched her belly with a secret smile.
Remember the pain of labour
as she struggled to give birth,
Held me against her swollen breast with joy.

Let her start again
from my first breath,
Return to find the child in me,
The awkward adolescent,
The middle aged woman
Who longs to be hugged.
Start the journey of our past
again.

'Are you sure dear?
I thought I had a son.

My Alzheimer's must have come to you as a shock,
Erasing a life in compliance with order.
You were utterly disappointed and in constant denial,
That my once elephantine memory faded into oblivion
Before your benevolent eyes.

Yet, the power of memory is never guaranteed
In the fading embers of life.

When I was in a global village of my own
You unstintingly lent me a hand.
And shadowed my altered life.

I became a stranger to you, my beloved family.
I know you had to embrace my new personality,
With all its trappings of change and demand and stress.
If I could turn back the great anvil of time...I would.

Sometimes I catch a glimpse of your smile
But I cannot respond.
You wait upon me hand and foot
Like the patience of a saint,
The door of your heart open without reserve.
Those happy moments we shared together.
When children played hide and seek in the vast garden.
When the clock was advanced,
During the evening study, all in mischief.
When we sat near the hearth during icy cold winter nights,
Stealing glimpses of the fire consuming the wattle logs,
Whilst reading our favourite books.
The exotic gold fish swimming the length and breadth of the tank.
Catching sight of a shooting star and making a wish.
You and I ageing with grace,
Our home now empty.
Our children like birds sprouting their reluctant wings
And flying off to distant lands.

Strangers After a Life Time Together
By Ravi Naicker

Therefore, cherish God's gift of memory, savour it,
Like you'd hug a snowman before the sunrise.

You look at me hoping for a response
But I stare at you like an old piece of furniture.
You weep and your tears cascade down your cheeks.
I weep and you wipe away my warm tears.
We look into each other's eyes
And memories of a life time gone by.
Sometimes I smile at nothing
And it's like manna to you.
I raise your hopes and I see your hopes defeated.
As our tears catch the light from the candle on the mantelpiece,
An enigma of life's chapters shucked.

I will perambulate the land and cross the seas to regain my memory.
I could not reciprocate your unconditional love.
You might imagine that I am not grateful,
But each day God watches your kind gestures,
Your selfless service – benedictions will come,
This is my fervent prayer.

There are so many questions with no answers.

It hadn't hit me, I wondered why -
it all seemed so surreal
until a memory melded in my mind
then formed in a tear

More teardrops formed fast
blurring up my eyes
those tricky tears of passage
they took me by surprise

Rivulets of teardrops trickled
I let them freely flow -
when we least expect it
our deepest feelings show.

Tears Of Passage
By Margaret O'Driscoll

That hot Sunday
he wanted the hedge cut very badly:
It must be done now, he said.
I said I'd do it when I was less busy
but that was too late for his paranoia
which was already muttering to him
that the *Evening Sentinel* would report him
for an overgrown hedge:
"Local Ex-Teacher's Hedge A Disgrace."
He reckoned the neighbours would spy on us
less easily with a trimmed hedge
(don't ask me how).

So he went out with secateurs, shears
and hacked at laurel and fir
as if they were the neighbours
and we couldn't stop him
even when he was in a sweat, trembling,
falling over, fitting, minor-stroking
on the ground, back in his chair,
his hands still jerkily pruning:
clip-clip-clip-clippety-clip,
paranoia still on his lips:
mustcutthehedgemustcutthehedge-
don'twanttheneighbourstoseethrough-
don'twantthepaperstoknow

and all I know now
is how un-busy I actually was
that hot Sunday.

My Father's Paranoia
By Jonathan Taylor

For my father

During those two hours of panic we should have known
we'd find him not dawdling over decking or azaleas
but in the car park, patting for keys, trying to get home.

Even before right hemisphere malfunction
everything outside his front door seemed mere detour
every excursion an annoying prelude to recursion,

holidays just delays, work a hanging-on the bell for lunch, tea;
at concerts his palms pushed down on chair arms
prepared for triumphal return of the home key.

But now, whether in living room from holiday, concert, work
or on family day out in Shropshire, he's permanently lost,
inside or out, his whole world a reduplicating car park.

Reduplicative Paramnesia, Shrewsbury Flower Show, 1997
By Jonathan Taylor

Seven

You saw it in an internet meme
You can't stand to talk on the phone
You're an over-stimulated introvert
And you want your friends to leave you alone.

You think you're OCD
You hate when things don't line up
If they offer desensitization therapy
You're sure to sign up.

You're very sensitive and
Sometimes you feel quite delicate
You say it isn't personal
When you have to fuck off for a bit.

Being an introvert doesn't automatically
Make you an antisocial psychopath
Just take a deep breath
And save your friends your wrath.

Anyway, I'm crazier than you
I never talk at parties.
I'm a social misfit
Everyone knows I'm a smarty.

I'm crazier than you
I hate all my friends
I have more diagnoses
And I get all the best meds.

I'm Crazier Than You
By Randall Horton

I have Seroquel, Xanax, and Trazadone
I take Klonopin, Effexor, and Haldol
All my pot and booze are gone
But prescriptions – I have them all.

I'm crazier than you.
I cry through greeting card ads.
I even lose control.
When puppies look sad.

I'm crazier than you.
I hate my whole family.
I beg them for love but tell them to
Fuck off when they want to see me.

I'm crazier than you
I watch Rick and Morty
You probably don't even understand this stanza
Because you're some kind of normy.

I'm crazier than you
I even think I'm a poet.
Who will lead change in the world
But know one will ever know it.

I'm crazier than you,
My therapist just resigned
She said I'm just too much.
I fear she may commit suicide.

I'm crazier than you
I'm the subject of a research protocol
I've donated my brain to science
Because I've no mind left at all.

I'm dancing on the air
I'm swinging on a tree
I'm flying through the sky
So high! So high!
This is me this is me!
Do you see?
Who was yesterday's lump
That grump
Clinging to the sofa
Crying for the dark?
Not me I swear it was not me
I know you asked her, kindly,
Coffee or tea?
And she shouted Don't Ask Just DO!
I remember I remember
But that was not me
It was another She
I swear.
This is me! This is me!
Dancing on the air
Swinging on a tree.

From Pole to Pole
By Jan McCarthy

For Kershia

> *The same scourge whips the joker and the enjoyer of the joke.*
> – Emerson, 'The Comic'

Take my advice, said the Parisian doctor:
mix in different circles, try Italian theatre.
This all-consuming melancholy, sir,
it's a mere spectre from your imagination.

Swallow these pills, by all means, sir,
but you also need to get out and about.
You're in Naples. Make the most of it,
seek out pleasurable society.

Go and see the great clown Carlini –
I hear he has the whole city in fits.
If your gloom can withstand his antics,
it must be incurable indeed.

Pagliacci
By Jonathan Taylor

He's sure to take you out of yourself,
sir, give life a humorous complexion,
help you to pull up your stockings
as I think they say back in England.

Carlini: he's your panacea, my friend.
He will make you laugh till you cry.
His jokes, they will split your sides
(again as the English sometimes say).

But it's no good, the patient said back:
I already go the Italian theatre nightly
because I am myself the great Carlini
and can hardly make myself laugh
except perhaps at my own misery.

Based on a story recounted by Ralph Waldo Emerson,
F. Wiseman, Charles Dickens, George Mikes and others.

Disappointment first stung when her
female form was pushed from the birth canal;
mother didn't give birth to a comedian.

Missing baptismal photos gave rise
to the quiet life she would lead,
a melancholy cast on her;
a security blanket worn
as a second skin well into her youth.

She first died when she was eight,
thrust into the epicentre of a divorce;
her thin veil of innocence
offered no protection.

In the aftermath she emerged muted,
a paler shade of herself,
a storage box for secrets of others.

She died for the second time at thirteen,
the thread of trust wound tightly around her body,
a chokehold about to unravel
sending her spinning into the world.

The Comedian
By Geraldine O'Kane

At eighteen she died for real,
her body imploding
as she fragmented out,
against those frowning upon her.

At twenty four she died for the last time,
seven years in exile
before a glint came upon her;
luminous dots sparked,
connected, reflected,
gestated inside her,
until she gave life to creativity.

Mother didn't give birth to a comedian,
she lost control and brandished a poet.

I'm not very good at this self love thing.

I always look for strangers,
thinking they could do it better,
and I don't post about it online,
I forget,
I'm no use,
that girl with the juice blender and the personal trainer is far ahead
of me –
that's why people pay her
to promote beauty products
so other people can buy them
and love themselves too.

Social Media Invented Self Love
By Isabelle Kenyon

The woods are quiet until
two Sika deer run out
white tails bobbing
a grey whippet in pursuit
the owner, the ghost of John Osborne
grunts a greeting and we talk about
his dog's inability to catch deer
despite he tells me, the animal's razor-sharp teeth.

We admire the view of the forest
the Norwegian Pines and Cedar Reds
before parting our separate ways.
He takes one road. I take mine.
I stroke the soft trunks of the Cedar Reds
and they whisper to me, everything will be ok.

On Coming Across Sika Deer
By Rachel Burns

Why bash your wings
against the glass,
draw blood;
why not turn around
see beauty behind,
to your left,
to your right.

Why can I not see
what you see -
that these questions
only exist outside
your reality

Futility
By Mike Gallagher

This morning my face is a seaside town in winter.
Eye-lid shutters nailed down, nostrils
salted. My nose a pickled whelk.
Stomach shrunk to a speckled pebble, bowels
donkey-kicking at wedged knees. Heart
a gull, trembling at the dawn.
There is a sign, thickly pasted, across my mouth:
                              Come Back in Spring.

Regret
By Jennie E. Owen

I do not need philosophers or priests to tell me so,
for I have climbed and rambled where the walkers go:
Cat Bells, Skiddaw, the Dales, the Chase,
Red Pike, the grit-stone face of Froggatt Edge.

With every climb there is a sense of leaving
behind. Not of the grieving kind,
for it touches something natural in man
to be outdoors and seeking higher ground,
to open the gate that leaves the road behind.

Rather, it is a finding, a reminder
of the grandeur of green and open space
and cloud-cottoned heights that touch steep skies,
where the larks and the lapwings weave
you into the natural scheme of things.

And always there is a looking down.
To see a lane meandering along the valley floor,
the tiny sheepdog in his yard
the farmhouse you can blot out with your thumb,
is to come to see yourself, to know
and to enjoy your littleness.

I smile when I remember
a certain rock to perch on, a spot beneath a tree,
a view where, by sitting still,
we begin to own it and are part of it.
And I think of climbing such a hill
or treading such a path, not as a going
but a kind of coming home,
a threshold crossed, a knowing,
that such a place, once owned, cannot be lost.

There is a Mystery to Life, Some Say.
By Bert Flitcroft

If I close my eyes, in this head space
I'll be able to concentrate on breathing.

The silver fish and woodlice can have
the corners underneath this bed;

I'll not care. I'll ignore the mustiness of
the orange nylon carpet, the dust on

the flock wallpaper, the pounding in
my neck. It won't be three in the morning,

with only a two bar electric fire and
The World Service for company.

These high walls with their empty picture
rail will disappear. The Victorian cornices

in which shadowy faces look down on me
will have to refocus, for I won't be here;

I'll be elsewhere.

Somewhere Else
By Jonathan Humble

The silent sand was in distress
Departed sea could not impress
No lonely tears could it cry
For the sun had baked it dry
No sparkle could it cajole
As spades dug deep, to its soul
The silent sand was in distress
Departed sea could not impress.

Grains of Life (Octelle)
By Jan Hedger

Winds howl and wail no mercy,
as you tumble and fall to the ground.
I run to catch you,
when you can no longer,
glide through the sky.

Once soft feathered and swift, now still.
Your warm heart, beating against my cupped palm,
as dead fear takes you.
I care. I wait.

My tears bathe your limp wings
and awakes a pain that cannot sleep.
Your empty perch, a silent song
that waits for dawn,
and you again will swoop and soar.

In the stillness of the misty morn
I pledge my undying love and set you free.

Silent Song
By Judith Carmody

Depression is a bird
with brain damage
from slamming
into your dining room window,
over

—slam—

and over

–slam–

again.
Hope may be Dickinson's thing
with the feathers, singing wordlessly
into the night but depression is the bird
flopping its broken wings, throwing itself
headlong into invisible barriers,
over and over again.
And when you think that it has stopped,
when you think that it has realized
that it cannot keep going,
it hits so hard that everything shatters.

A Bird With Broken Wings
By Kelsi Rose

I have been cradled within the evergreen arms of the biggest Scots pine
and I have recovered.
I have swam in the coldest of currents with battling brownies too elusive for any rod
and I have recovered.
I have flown on the backs of ospreys for miles to far and distant eyries
and I have recovered.
I have dunked heid into the icy depths of lochs on the earliest of midge mad mornings
and I have recovered.
I have dragged fingers and toes through the soft sands of those golden Highland beaches
and I have recovered.
I have walked barefoot through burns, rivers and streams that have shone, glimmered and gleamed
and I have recovered.
I have sat perfectly still on the windiest of hills as the gusts played my ribs like an xylophone
and I have recovered.
I have clambered and climbed up mystical mountains that have given me the time to be heard
and I have recovered.
I have ran with the stags to the edges of crumbling crags in valleys so hidden you would have a better chance of finding Wally
and I have recovered.
I have stopped, stood and listened to nature's sonorous symphony unmastered without headphones nor speakers
and I have recovered.
Often I have sought refuge amongst the Scottish wilderness
Ma nature, my Scottish therapist.

Ma Nature, My Therapist
By Greg Robertson

I look outward and I see:

dogs.

Thousands of dogs, bounding towards me, from the tiny terrier growing larger, bigger in my eyeline until they become massive German Shepherds and Rottweilers, every breed you can imagine, dogs.

From a bird's eye, I look like a human eye, built of dogs and their dark eyes. I am the central pupil to an iris of browns, beige, flecks of white and fluff. Following vein trails of more dogs.

There are so many dogs.

They jump onto me. I am surrounded by dogs. Dogs in my arms, dogs clambering up my leg, sitting in the crevice behind my knee. Dogs on my head. Dogs on my shoulders. Dogs I am wearing as a jacket and trousers, accompanied by a fluffy puppy belt. I am covered, I am drowning, in a sea of happy, waggy dogs.

I look to the floor and I see:

dogs.

Two dogs. Small, toy sized, Bishon Freische dogs. These two dogs are swirling and snuffling at my feet. My feet bark at them. My feet are dogs.

My lap is a lap dog. I am a giant dog. Made of dogs.

With a pathetically weak "woof", I am brought back.

I attach a lead onto my crippled, affected dog. She trips as I take her outside.

Dogs
By Bethan Rees

'I'm slipping away a bit at a time...
and all I can do is watch it happen'
-Terry Pratchett

It is out in the garden by the flower bed,
by an empty shed, you try to water some flowers.

Your hand like a closed rosebud, delicate, trembling,
holding a watering can. Your mouth open, a quivering

lip, asking the sky questions & the sky answers in drops,
dancing, falling, crawling down your cheek across your back

to your feet. You try to water some flowers, but you forget
why you are here, why you are there, you forget birthdays,

family, yesterday. You forget who you are in the rain
by the shed in the garden, & the scent of the roses

& the murmur of the vine, makes your lip quiver
& your hand bloom, dropping the watering can

in the rain, by the flower bed, by an empty shed,
you ask a rose who you are & the sky answers in drops.

Conversation with a Rose
By Stephen Byrne

Even a shot of WD40,
didn't stop her wheel creaking.
The noise made her ears twitch
as if she'd been electrocuted.

My hamster was not one
for giving up. Her little legs
kept running on that bloody
wheel, until it broke.

She dragged her flabby body
to a corner, crouched and folded
in on herself, a blackish-grey
mound of fluff.

When my husband stuck his finger,
through the wiry bars and poked
her to perform, she didn't know
how to tell him – she was broken.

My Hamster's Depression
By Anne Walsh Donnelly

With a curious mind
I turn,
Watch the waves
Crash against my shore.

I stay,
Search for the silence
Hidden within the pounding rhythm
Of chaos and fear.

I sink into the earth,
Spread my roots,
Welcome the rushing water
As the waves come and go.

Just for this moment,
This breath,
My pain washes away
And I hear the space between sounds.

The Space between Sounds
By Emma Mooney

Eight

I meditated this morning.

Trying to find a bigger space
In the smaller space I currently inhabit.

Hours become heavy with illness.

The light lasts longer
yet seems much further away.

The breath helps.

But it's the first coffee
that reassures me.

I am still alive.

I cried yesterday
and the day before.

Though it's not all Eeyore.

There is beauty too.

Minutes of deep appreciation
for the love in friends and family and myself
to tidy the fear away.

And books and words and TV.

Though when I watch yet another episode of dodgy American sci-fi
the other voice in my head keeps showing up to remind me
it's not a fucking holiday.

Staycation
By Melissa Jacob

For Nicole, a villanelle

Ask yourself, honestly, 'am I happy?'
Lie on the damp grass, in your favourite spot
Peer through the spindle of an ash tree

So as to interrogate the grey sky
You are not hungry, or freezing, but
Ask yourself, honestly, 'am I happy?'

The birds don't seem to be, they merely fly
And the leaves, they just hang there, shot
Peer through the spindle of an ash tree

Of the tortured branches, seek a reply
Go on, I know you must do it a lot
Ask yourself, honestly, 'am I happy?'

Seek the answer throughout the galaxy
From alpha to omega, dot to dot
Peer through the spindle of an ash tree

Deep down you know it's pointless really
Because, if you have to ask you are not
Peer through the spindle of an ash tree
Ask yourself, honestly, 'am I happy?'

Am I Happy?
By William Hatchett

Have hope and be strong,
but don't let your hope run away with you,
you'll only be disappointed in the end.

Laugh loud and play hard,
but not so much with the drink and drugs.

Live in the moment,
but a bit of a forward plan might be worth considering.

Smile often; dream big,
but remember that smiling at the wrong time can be perceived as
being arrogant
and uncaring.
If you dream be ready to still smile when those dreams are smashed.

Remember you are loved...
and hated in equal measure- but one balances out the other so that's
kind of
okay.

And never, ever, give up,
unless it's genuinely futile- then perhaps try something else?

Positives
By Andrew Barnes

Into the darkness,
Into my biggest fears,
I died,
But do not stand at my grave and cry,
For it was the parts of me that I no longer needed,
It was my burdens that diminished,
It was my mind that gave up the fight,
My ego loosened its hold in a flood of tears,
Sobbing that it had had enough of trying to control everything.

In my exhaustion I surrendered to the light and let all else burn
away,
Some would look on and call it destruction,
But the truth is it is a purification,
Rising from the ashes.

I have to play out the same outdated patterns until I finally get sick
of it,
Some would look on and call it madness,
Taking a step backwards,
But my soul knows it is necessary,
To fall apart at times so I can reassemble,
To shatter, disintegrate and let my heart burst open,
So that the real me can be free, can be seen and has space to
breathe,
To receive.

And really see in clarity,
With all these layers surrounding me I felt suffocated,
I could not see my own beauty,
As the ties that bound me trapped me in a web of my own creation,
It was necessary to feel the push and pull of worries,
Not knowing which direction to go in,
So I could come back into stillness and find myself,

Into the Darkness I Died
By Aiyana Rosel

To unhook so I'm free to move,
To stretch and expand once more,
I am free to transform,
To show you more of what I am capable of,
That I am so much stronger than the victim I perceived myself to be
in the past.

The past is no longer, it doesn't exist except as a memory feedback
loop,
An echo of what has been, it need not control us any longer,
For there is just this now to stand my ground knowing what I have to
give the world,
That I have value,

Sometimes we lose sight of our worthiness,
Under the conditioning of an unattainable perfection,
That to have a beautiful body is to be whole,
A goal that leaves you feeling empty and unfulfilled, that no matter
how hard you try you will never fulfill the perfect form that society
has conditioned into you,
But when we are tapped into our souls true power we realise that we
are so much more than just this body, our vessel,
Infinitely brighter than just this body of yours,
And yet your body is your valued treasure, unique and beautiful in all
its flaws.

Hold that body of yours tightly and love it knowing it is yours,
And a way of expressing your soul in form,
Let it be an expression of your radiance within,
Who cares if you your hair is a little messy, let yourself be wild and
untamed,
For a soul like yours could never be contained,
Let your movements be an expression of your fierce spirit,
Prowling with the strength of a lion,
Ready in waiting, you look serene when really you are just waiting to
pounce, to spring into action at a moment's notice,
For once you have shed the burdens you feel a new lightness you
haven't felt before,
To return,
To yourself.

I stop writing
and my life falls apart
as if that smashing
of a wrecking ball
into a building
splinters of me fly out
and everybody runs for cover
because they don't want to be burdened
with my pain

but you have to get through that pain

to fully appreciate
that whatever physical pressures are placed
upon your body
your mind can remain clear
the strength is in your beliefs
and you have to steer
the ship of your destiny
and now
I start to write

storm clouds part
and I can see
chinks of light appearing.

Silver Lining
By Katie Lewington

Walk in the park
by the lake
where the peddle boats
trundle over
smooth water
go buy
an easy-to-read book
follow the sentences
to a place of safety
rest under the laburnum
its great yellow
hanging over you
think of those
who you loved
take time to breathe
watch the pigeon
crooked head
busy with questions
take time to
flay your anger
take time to
reach out your hand,
take time out
for the big dreaming
let the years float past
let go of the years
take time out
take time.

Take Time Out
By Catherine Whittaker

Are cormorants born with the theory of
refraction or do they learn to hunt
by mirrors?

How you see around corners
through your tears,
always makes me feel that wonder
of a child.

There have been day when oceans have been
dripping off my wings,
my stomach singing tunes.

Then I was fed by you.

I traced a map to our house on your back,
while you felt my gravity pulling through you.

I shall not be afraid when I am lost.
I shall not be afraid when I am lost.

I hear there are some good theories on
why we talk about love,
when the world needs our gratitude,
when the world is burning some streets along,

making the sunset sweeter,
when the words shoal for feeding.

Simple Physics
By Christopher Hopkins

Moving always.
Mixed business and holidays.
Right by night,
Write by candlelight.
Writhe in hot sheets,
Skin scratched from fresh mosquito bites.
No privacy.
Music by piracy.
Pariah dog passively patrol the streets.
Keep possessions in sight,
Cows and goats with hips slight.
Hop on the killer bus until the beach where we all alight.

Love is everywhere.
But lust is in more places.
The hills change, the skies change, but never the faces.
We're all just filling out free spaces.
Then get replaced and wait by the road, with heads strewn and badly
packed cases.
Minds unmade like hotel beds
And my soul is still in shreds.
I see the local families move,
Like ships in distant directions.
I see myself in their eyes but its only reflections.
Across continents-
Trying for constant contentment.
If happiness was measurable is there enough to go around?
And can I cash it in when I float up from the gravelly ground?

Travel
By Abbie Logan

Swapped cattle for goats,
Instead of dogs–
Cats wait for fishing boats.
And they stack squid into boxes and measure their catches and move
past the embering piles of ashes.
No home.
Just trying to belong,
Hum old yogi mantra songs,
Watch local families in crowded throngs.
Tabula rasa.
Each new mind an empty wrapper,
Sweet or sour comes from the soul and it's all that really matters.

Listen therapist - we need to talk
There are things you don't see with your brief therapy
and half a dozen sessions before you set me free.
With your emphasis on illness and diagnosis;
hoarding symptoms like stamp collectors after an illusive Penny
Black.
You medicalise social problems, like they're our fault
but we cannot be wished away
Are we ill because we're depressed or is it because we're oppressed?
And is the key to this oppression being robbed of self expression?

And there's a riot in my head -
but just like Martin Luther King said, "Riots are conversations of the
voiceless".
And 'we' lost our voice because 'you' usurped our language.
Lets take the term 'recovery'
For health professionals like you it becomes
an excuse to cease treatment, eliminate resources;
deny us the 'luxury' of difference.
In your hands, the Langue has no Parole*

But 'we' invented the term 'recovery'
as a way to understand our difficulties.
It's how we hold onto the past and recover identity.
It stops us being written off - just as Lord Byron Said,
"Deformity is daring...", and we strive to make good, catch up
and maybe overtake those who have not felt the pain of emotional
overload.
And as we re-calibrate our pain we echo Kurt Cobain
when he wrote, "Thank you for the tragedy. I need it for my art"

*Barthes, R. (1972). Mythologies

'Recovery' won 2nd prize in the Disability Arts Cymru (DAC) inaugural poetry
competition (2015).

Recovery
By Des Mannay

The therapy session lies behind
dank Victorian garden wall
graffitied with squiggles of silver.
The therapy session is waiting beyond
cones and pipes and builders.
The therapy centre's waiting room
is set next to the kitchen.
I hear aluminium sinks
rippled by taps that stutter
between the creak of clock hands
always edging closer to
the minute of full disclosure.

Therapy Session
By Roy Moller

Yellow teeth have tasted tobacco,
scarred skin has felt the knife,
grey hairs have withstood life:

Fearfully and wonderfully weathered.

Calloused fingers have pressed the strings,
cracked bones have tried utterly,
bruised wrists have broken free:

Fearfully and wonderfully blemished.

Faltering feet know they have strayed,
dejected eyes have been accused,
Yet contrite hearts shall not be refused:

Fearfully and wonderfully stained.

Secure voices can resonate devotion,
crooked limbs have been reset,
repeating lips do not forget:

Fearfully and wonderfully re-made.

Made
By Peter Lilly

Victory
is getting out of bed, even though
it is past noon and everyone walking past
has seen that your curtains are
still closed.

Victory
is having curtains in the first place,
and a net behind them, and
space to put them up and
keeping them there.

Victory
is those sharp clean teeth and that cereal
that you swallow down and keep down
and the milk that is still OK to drink,
today.

Victory
is remembering that above those sharp
teeth are lips that kiss, that shape
soft words:
you are allowed.

Invicted

By SM. Jenkin

Victory
is those clothes that keep you warm,
and those matching yellow socks
that remind you of
summer beaches.

Victory
is making it beyond the chipped
front door today, and staying put
when they walk past, and see
right through you.

Victory
is not telling them to go
fuck themselves, because really.
Who knows what their victory looks like;
is it anything like yours?

Victory
is going to bed and staying there,
not knowing if tomorrow is going to
be a victory day and
doing it anyway.

The nightmare stinks;
there is blood on the pillow,
sweat on the sheets.
Porridge is sweet
with raisins and honey,
but mugs of Yorkshire Tea
are cracked,
apple skin wrinkled,
flesh is mushy.
Cold brick, hard floors,
oil paint flaking,
hot lamps, popped bulbs,
damp clothes drying.
I hope by tea-time to forget
I have woken up crying,
By evening, comfort comes
with olive oil, garlic, chicken
and gin, tonic, ice and lemon,
gin, tonic, ice and lemon.

Come, Smell My Home
By Janet Dean

Be brave my girl
though life's a swirl
of change and fear
I'm always near
in all unknown
you're not alone
just come to mum
if you are glum
I'll listen well
to what you tell
no matter what
to every jot
the good and bad
troubles you had
leave them with me
then you'll see
the way to go
I won't say no
I'm here for you
in all you do.

Be Brave My Girl
A message to my daughter now and in the future if she's ever anxious.
By Emma Major

Poet Biographies

Abbie Logan has been writing since she was 7 and has always maintained a passion for poetry and written word. She has never been published but writes more for the release and expression. Having travelled extensively around Asia, she has found it to be the best way to capture the world at large. She currently resides as a chef in Edinburgh.

Adrian McRobb has been writing for 30 years and is a founding member of Cramlington Writers Group. He is a Performance Poet, and the past holder of the Lowford Trophy. Adrian has performed his work, at Open-Mics in Morpeth and Newcastle.

Aiyana Rosel is a registered healthcare professional with a degree in Psychology, based in the UK. Her passions are helping people, promoting peace and writing. She shares her poetry on her Facebook page 'Aiyana Rosel' and writes a blog about her adventures into spirituality and consciousness on 'A Personal Spiritual Journey'. She has a vision and mission to help people heal their mind, body and spirit to reach their full potential.

Alan Savage comes from Middlesbrough in Teesside, UK, and currently lives in Cippenham, Slough. Alan works as a secondary English teacher and likes to write verse/poetry as an obsessive compulsive hobby (meaning he can't really stop himself!) Alan has written a series of poems called 'The Teesside Verses', available online as a downloadable PDF and is currently writing a collection of poems aimed at children. Alan is happily married with two children and a dog.

Alison Down is an award winning Liverpool based performance poet, screenwriter and dramaturg.

Andrew Barnes is developing his reputation as a poet through publication of work in a range of literary magazines, and through performance including regular readings at Kitchen Garden cafe Kings Heath and on Internet Radio Wildfire.

Andy Horwood is a self published poet, who started writing poetry to deal with his mental health and never stopped. He has covered themes such as love, gender identify and mental health in his poems and has been published in anthologies.

Andy Humphrey was born in the Wirral and now lives in York where he works as a legal adviser with individuals who are homeless or facing loss of their homes, a great many of whom have suffered serious mental ill health. For 10 years he has been MC of The Speakers' Corner open mic in York and he has published two collections of poetry, A Long Way to Fall (Lapwing, 2013) and Satires (Stairwell Books, 2015). Much of his poetic output uses the timeless language of nature, myth and fairytale to tell stories with a contemporary relevance.
Website: http://andyhumphrey1971.webs.com.

Andy N is a writer and sound artist from Manchester, UK. He is the Author of 'Return to Kemptown' and 'The End of Summer'. His website is: Andy N – Writer and Experimental Musician

Angela Topping is the author of eight poetry collections and four chapbooks. Her work has featured on BBC Radio's Poetry Please and she is a former writer in residence at Gladstone's Library. Angela Topping's latest collection is 'The Five Petals of Elderflower' (Red Squirrel Press).

Anna Kander is a writer in the Midwestern US. She trained as a psychotherapist and remains licensed to practice. Her first book, 'Slide a Mirror to Me', is forthcoming from Transcendent Zero Press. Her poetry and fiction have appeared in Gone Lawn, Ellipsis, Train, and other magazines. Find her at http://annakander.com

Anna Matyjiw has been writing poetry and Lyrics since 2009 and has worked as a Performance Poet.

Anne Walsh Donnelly lives in Mayo, Ireland with her two teenage children. She writes short fiction and poetry. Her work has previously been published in various print and online magazines such as Crannog, The Blue Nib, Star82 Review and Cold Coffee Stand. Her poems were highly commended in the Over The Edge New Writer of the Year Award (2017) and commended in the Westport Arts Festival poetry competition (2017). She sometimes writes about her own experience of depression and hopes these poems resonate with readers and contribute to raising awareness around mental health. Anne would like to dedicate her poem in this anthology to anyone who has ever felt like her little hamster.

Avantika Singhal is a poetess and spoken word artist living in Jaipur, India. Over the course of her writing career, she has gotten her poetry published in respected literary magazines such as Writer's Asylum, Red Fez, Textploit, Jabberwock Online, The Indian Review, Spillwords, Emerald Hues Anthology, Hall Of Poets-Valentine Anthology, United We Stand: Poets Against Terror Anthology, Parasva Anthology, Germ Magazine, Pressure Gauge Press and Our Poetry Archive etc. She aspires to make a positive impact with her writing. She has also contributed her literary creations to a bedtime story book named Tales By Teens, online platforms like Half Baked Beans and Indian Women Blog. She hopes to start studying English Literature at Regent's University, London soon.

Barbara Derbyshire is an author of short fiction and poetry. Originally from London and now an Irish citizen, her home is in Kerry where, with more time to think, observe and remember, she has rediscovered her love of writing. Her first published book is 'Tapestry of Love, Life and Spirit', and, together with other writers from North Kerry and West Limerick, she has contributed to the anthology, 'Striking A Chord'.

Barry Fentiman Hall is a Medway based poet of place, even if that place is sometimes between his ears. He has been published in a number of journals such as Crack The Spine, Anti Heroin Chic, and Picaroon. His first solo pamphlet 'The Unbearable Sheerness Of Being' came out on Wordsmithery in 2016, which he recently performed as a solo show at Sheppey Little Theatre. He is also the editor of Confluence Magazine. He likes cats and has an affinity with hares.

Bert Flitcroft grew up in Lancashire and is a graduate of Sheffield University. He is an experienced and accomplished poet who has two collections of poetry published: 'Thought-Apples' with Offa's Press and 'Singing Puccini at the Kitchen Sink' with Fineleaf. He was Staffordshire Poet Laureate 2015-2017 and curated 'The Staffordshire Poetry Collection' which is now available on-line. In 2015 he was Poet in Residence at The Southwell Poetry Festival, and in 2016 at The Shire Hall Gallery, Recently he has been Resident Poet at The Wedgwood Museum and The Brampton Museum and Gallery in Newcastle.

Bethany Gordon grew up in a small village and often wrote poetry with her Grandfather. Now in her mid-twenties, Bethany has continued to write after the loss of her Grandparents, and has performed on local radio, regular open mic nights, as well as the finale night of a mental health arts cabaret. She is currently working on her first book. Writing every day, Bethany uploads to her Instagram page @bethrosewrites, with a typewritten vintage-style, lost letters approach to poetry and spoken word.

Bethan Rees is fairly new to the poetry scene and thoroughly enjoys her time as a friend of Poetry Swindon. She is currently studying an MSc in Creative Writing for Therapeutic Purposes and hopes to travel workshops in the future. Although now living in Swindon, Bethan grew up in Neath, South Wales and spent some time living in South Dakota, USA. Her favourite things are words, nuzzes and her useless, ancient dog Mitzie.

Carla Stein has been published in Sustenance, an anthology (release date: October, 2017), Ascent Aspirations Magazine, An Anthology of Nanaimo Poetry, and Island Woman Magazine. She regularly reads at a variety of venues on Vancouver Island and has produced her first chapbook titled, 'Sideways Glances of an Everyday Sailor'. She is a member of the Federation of BC Writers and a board member of Wordstorm Society of the Arts. Carla recently completed a poetry course with Fiona Lam and Evelyn Lau through Simon Fraser University as well as a course through the University of Iowa Writer's Studio. Until leaving the field to re-focus on writing, she worked as an accredited mental health and addictions counselor. She holds a Masters of Education degree and a diploma in Fine Art. Her career path previously included writing as both a freelance and broadcast journalist.

Carole Bromley has three books with Smith/Doorstop, the most recent being 'Blast Off!', a collection for children. www.carolebromley.co.uk

Carrie Danaher Hoyt is a life-long lover and writer of poetry. It is her humble opinion that poetry is the highest form of human communication. Poems (she says) at once highlight what is unique and what is universal in humanity. Carrie lives in Massachusetts where she is a wife and mother of three school-aged kids. To pay the bills (as her poems don't yet do this) she works as an estate planning attorney. Beside family and poetry, she loves travel, volunteer work and concerts. You can read more of Carrie's poems published by Twitterization Nation, www.twitterization.wordpress.com and @ nationOtwits and follow her on Twitter @CDanaherH

Cathy Whittaker has had a sequence of 15 poems published in Quintet, Cinnamon Press. Her work has also appeared in Under the Radar, Prole, The Interpreters House, Envoi, Orbis, Ink Sweat and Tears, Southlight, Obessed with Pipework, The Magnolia Review, Mslexia, and many other magazines and anthologies. She was shortlisted for the Bridport Prize. She won the Southport Writers Competition and was runner up for The Baker Prize. Cathy is a tutor in Creative Writing.

Charley Reay is a Newcastle based writer from the Lincolnshire Fens. Her poems are published by Obsessed With Pipework, Ink, Sweat & Tears, and Three Drops Press among others. She also performs on the North East spoken word scene.
You can find her on Twitter @charleyreay

Cheryl Pearson lives and writes in Manchester. Her poems have appeared in publications including The Guardian, Southword, Under The Radar, and Frontier. In 2017 she won the Torbay Poetry Competition, and was awarded second prize in the Cannon Poets Competition. Her first collection, 'Oysterlight', is available now from Pindrop Press.

Christopher Hopkins grew up in Neath, South Wales during the 1970's surrounded by a landscape of machines and mountains. Christopher currently resides in the Canterbury area with his wife and baby daughter and works for NHS cancer services. His debut chapbook 'Take Your Journeys Home' has been released with Clare Songbirds Publishing House, New York and his second is due out in Spring 2018. He has been nominated for IPPY book award for poetry and has been nominated twice the for Pushcart Prize (2018) for his poems 'Sorrow on the Hill' and 'Smoke and Whiskey'. Christopher has had numerous publications including The Morning Star Newspaper. His spoken word poetry has also featured in a podcast of Golden Walkmen Magazine.

Colin Dardis is a poet, editor and freelance arts facilitator from Northern Ireland. His work has been widely published throughout Ireland, UK and USA. Colin co-runs Poetry NI is the editor of FourXFour and Lagan Online, and was one of Eyewear Publishing's Best New British and Irish Poets 2016. A collection with Eyewear, 'The X of Y', is forthcoming in 2018. www.colindardispoet.co.uk

Connie Ramsay Bott grew up in Michigan, where many of her poems and stories take place. She teaches Creative Writing courses with a colleague (openmindwriting.com). Her novel Girl Without Skin was published by Cinnamon Press in September 2017.

CR Smith has been published both online and in print. You can find examples here https://crsmith2016.wordpress.com and instagram.com/smith.cr/@smith.cr and Twitter: @carolrosalind

Dave Kavanagh lives and writes in a small fishing village in North Count Dublin. His work includes poetry, prose & short fiction. Dave has had work been recently published online at, Fourth & Sycamore, Algebra of Owls, Taxicab and others. His poetry has recently been included in the anthologies Poetry Soup (International Poetry Foundation) and Indelible Poets. Dave is originator and co-editor of The Blue Nib.

D. E. Kerr writes confessional poetry and fiction within Melbourne, Australia, on a phone, laptop, scrawled in notebooks, or on napkins - whatever she can find to write upon. Her debut poetry collection, 'Carnival Games', will be released in 2018. You can find her on instagram (d.e.kerr), facebook (D. E. Kerr) or twitter (@d_e_kerr) for updates on her work.

Des Mannay is the winner of the rethinkyourmind poetry competition (2015). He is the 'Gold Award' winner in the Creative Futures Literary Awards (2015), and was shortlisted for the Erbacce prize for poetry (2015, and 2016), Welsh Poetry Competition (2015), The John Tripp and Idris Davies poetry competition; as well as being part of the Rhymney Valley Literature and Arts Festival 2016, and the Disability Arts Cymru poetry Competition (2016). He has poems published in I Am Not A Silent Poet online journal, The Angry Manifesto, Proletarian Poetry, Yellow Chair Review, Indiana Voice Journal, Stand Up And Spit, Red Poets, The Scum Gentry and work in a number of poetry anthologies. Des is on Facebook as 'The stuff wot I wrote' Des Mannay - Hooligan Poet and Twitter as @hooliganpoet

Earl. J. Guernsey Jr. was born in Syracuse, NY. He has been writing poetry and fiction since his early childhood days, many of which got published in local school magazines and journals. He published his first poem when he was nine when he won a local newspaper contest. His poetry is a reflection of his lifelong struggle with mental illness. A platform of which he uses to raise awareness about mental health and to advocate for better mental health services.

Eddie Carter writes mainly about insomnia, depression, lost love and how the modern working day can leave you feeling low. For Eddie, writing is therapeutic and a way of coping with depression. Eddie blogs at: http://gluebagsandlostlove.blogspot.co.uk/

Eduardo Escalante is a writer and researcher living in Valparaíso, Chile. He publishes regularly in Hispanic Reviews (Signum Nous, Nagari, Espacio Luke, Lakuma Pusaki, Sur Revista de Literatura, Revista Ariadna, Aurora Boreal, among others) and also in Spillwords, Slamchop, Writer Resist, Constellations, Peacock Journal (forthcoming), Adelaide Literary Magazine and, Gramma Poetry. His writing tells stories with a contemporary relevance and he write poems everyday.

Eithne Cullen was born in Dublin; her family moved to London when she was six years old. She has taught in East London secondary schools for 37 years. An avid reader, Eithne takes great pleasure from her reading group, which encourages an eclectic mix of books. She likes to write stories and poems and is a member of Forest Poets and Write Next Door writing groups. She lives with her husband in East London, is unashamedly proud of her three grown up children and endeavours to embarrass them as often as she can.

Eithne Lannon is a native of Dublin, Ireland. She's been widely published in various magazines such as Boyne Berries, The Ogham Stone, Skylight 47, Stanzas, The Limerick Magazine and FLARE. On-line she's published with Sheila-na-Gig, Headstuff, Barehands, BeZine, Tales from the Forest, A New Ulster and The Galway Review among others. She was Artist in Residence in Loughshinny Boathouse, Co. Dublin, during the summer of 2016.

Emma Lee has most recently published the book 'Ghosts in the Desert' (IDP, 2015). She co-edited 'Over Land, Over Sea: poems for those seeking refuge' (Five Leaves, 2015) and reviews for poetry journals and on her blog http://emmalee1.wordpress.com

Emma Major has been writing poetry since childhood but only started sharing it online in her 30s when she started writing poems about depression and baby loss. She writes in many poetic forms from haiku and cinquain to free prose, taking the lead from the subject matter and her emotions. She has written two collections of poetry 'This is my story, this is my song' and 'An alphabet of mental health' and has had poems included in two poetry anthologies. Emma is currently working on a book of poetry and reflections about her recent loss of eye sight due to a neurological condition.

Emma Mooney is a poet and novelist. Her novels, 'A Beautiful Game' and 'Wings to Fly' are published by Crooked Cat Books. She is currently completing her Master in Creative Writing at the University of Stirling and is working on her third novel. Emma believes passionately in giving everyone a voice. Find out more at www.emmamooney.co.uk

Emma Page was born and brought up in the Midlands, and has been writing since she was old enough to hold a pen. A politically active law graduate with a massive case of wanderlust, Emma has lived in both Italy and Jamaica. She performs at spoken word events and after a life-long wrestling match with depression and anxiety, the theme of mental health is a subject close to her heart.

Faatima Saleem is a 20 year old student at the University of Salford, currently studying Drama and Creative Writing. Faatima has been writing poetry for over two years online and more recently reading poetry at various different venues. Faatima's work often explores the elements and nature.

F.A. Peeke is a poet from South London. She began to explore her passion for writing at the tender age of seven and has been attempting to express a version of events through her eyes ever since, whether that be through her poetry, lyrics or photojournalistic exploits. Her debut poetry collection is due out in February 2018, called 'Crossing Paths' and will be available to buy on Amazon. You

can also join the author on her popular Instagram page: @f.a.peeke
or at her website: www.fapeeke.com

Finola Scott is a Slam winning granny whose poems are widely
published in anthologies and magazines including And Other
Poems, Obsessed with Pipework, The Ofi Press and Clear Poetry. Liz
Lochead was her mentor on Glasgow's Clydebuilt Scheme.

Galya Varna is a poet, book reviewer and visual artist. Born in
Varna, the summer capital of Bulgaria, on the Black Sea Coast, Galya
Varna now lives in Greece, on the coast of the Aegean Sea. She has
been writing poetry, short stories and plays for many years and is
currently working on her first poetry book to be published at the
beginning of 2018. Some of her poems are freely available on her
blog www.galyavarna.wordpress.com. Galya is also the driving force
behind the new creative project WeArtFriends and the bimonthly
online magazine Doorway to Art. Galya Varna holds a MA in English
literature and linguistics and language acquisition is another passion
of hers. For many years she used to work in the area of social work,
setting up and managing services in Bulgaria and South Eastern
Europe for adults and children with mental health issues. You can
contact Galya Varna on Twitter @GalyaVarna; Blog www.galyavarna.
wordpress.com and through the website www.we-art-friends.com

Geraldine O'Kane is a poet, creative writing facilitator and mental
health advocate. Her work has been published in numerous
anthologies, journals and zines in Ireland, the UK and the US,
most recently Arlen House, Eyewear Publishing, Flare Magazine,
and Poems in Profile. Her manuscript was recently shortlisted for
the 2017 Melita Hume poetry prize. Geraldine is co-host of Purely
Poetry, a monthly poetry open mic night, run in partnership with
the Crescent Arts Centre. Currently she is working towards her
first full collection of poetry and was a recipient of the Artist Career
Enhancement Scheme (ACES) 2015/16 from the Arts Council of
Northern Ireland.

Genevieve Glynn is a twenty one year old poet currently living in Liverpool. Her poem for this anthology is about depression and the knock on effect it has on loved ones. It was inspired by Bed by Tracy Emin which Genevieve saw displayed in the Tate Liverpool - she couldn't help but see the resemblance between the work and the spaces occupied by loved ones.

Glen Wilson lives and works in Portadown, Co Armagh. He has been widely published having work in The Honest Ulsterman, Foliate Oak, Iota, Southword and The Incubator Journal amongst others. In 2014 he won the Poetry Space competition and was shortlisted for the Wasafiri New Writing Prize. He won the Seamus Heaney Award for New Writing 2017. He is currently working on his first collection of poetry.

Greg Robertson is a removal porter and a poet from sunny Leith, Scotland. He picked up poetry through a love of language and self expression, revelling in the power of the word both written and spoken. This is his first publication.

Harriet Cooper was born in Solihull Hospital, screaming, 1985. Loves the colour purple, hates energy drinks; discovered the art of writing as a means of self-expression, via Bradgate Writers group. Her work is published in 'A Visitor Calls' an Arts Council England funded anthology (edited by Lydia Towsey and Peter Buckley) and recently featured as part of an installation exploring mental health and detention, created by artist and writer, David Parkin. Harriet is committed to challenging stigma, a subject close to her heart as a result of her own personal experience and many diagnoses. Loves the sunshine and being around water; the dog, Sonny - and beaches.

Hilary Robinson lives in Saddleworth and is a retired primary school teacher. She has had work published in The Interpreter's House, Obsessed with Pipework, Avis, Strix and Riggwelter. Her poetry has been included in several anthologies such as 'A New Manchester Alphabet' (Manchester Writing School 2015) and 'Noble Dissent' (Beautiful Dragons Press 2017). Hilary has recently completed her MA in Creative Writing at Manchester Metropolitan University. Since coming to poetry writing late in life, Hilary is trying to cram in as much of it as she can and will often be found at readings, workshops and launches. You can follow her on Twitter (@Hilro1) or on her occasional blog (mamierob.wordpress.com).

Hilary Walker began writing poetry at the suggestion of a friend and now enjoys writing and performing poetry on a regular basis. Hilary believes that within her poetry she creates a space of honesty that is difficult to find in any other aspect of her life. She writes passionately about life experiences in order to understand and make sense of the world. The poem featured in this anthology has recently been made into a video available on You Tube under Poet Mark Mace Smith.

Jade Moore is a freelance writer, journalist and poet living in Beeston, Nottingham. She uses poetry as a form of therapy to deal with her anxiety and relationship with her body. Often poetry is the best way for her voice to be heard, and she is steadily navigating Nottingham's spoken word scene. Her poems have appeared in oneiroi zine, Small Acts of Kindness Anthology, and Christmas Zine Vol. 2 published by Mud Press. Blogger at: advocateofbooks. wordpress.com

Jane Burn is a North East based artist and writer originally from South Yorkshire. Her poems have been featured in magazines such as The Rialto, Under The Radar, Butcher's Dog, Iota Poetry, And Other Poems, The Black Light Engine Room and many more, as well as anthologies from the Emma Press, Beautiful Dragons, Poetry Box, Emergency Poet and Kind of a Hurricane Press. Her pamphlets include Fat Around the Middle, published by Talking Pen and Tongues of Fire published by the BLER Press. Her first full collection, 'nothing more to it than bubbles' has been published by Indigo Dreams. She also established the poetry site The Fat Damsel. She was longlisted in the 2014 & 2016 National Poetry Competition.

Janet Dean lives in York. She has been shortlisted in the Bridport Prize and commended in the Stanza Poetry Competition. Most recently, her poems have been published in magazines and anthologies by Ariadne's Thread, Paper Swans Press, The Morning Star, Templar Poetry and Clear Poetry. In 2016 she co-edited 'The Friargate Anthology' which was launched at the York Literature Festival, and in 2017 her poems appeared in The York Literary Review and The Valley Press Anthology of Yorkshire Poetry.

Jan Hedger started writing children's poetry in 2001 and this grew into what it is today, a diverse mix of dancing trees, to the reality of war, from deep emotion to gentle humour. Jan believes poetry should be accessible to all and one of her greatest joys is performing her poetry. Jan has self published 2 poetry books –'Words in Imagination' and 'On Calico Wings', and in 2013 produced, designed & printed 'Our Friends & Their Habitats Near & Far' - an animal poetry book. Jan is on the steering committee for the Wilfred Owen festival to be held in Oswestry in Nov 18'.

Jan McCarthy is a Mind member from the Black Country. She was a finalist for the Asham Literary Award 2011. She writes novels, poetry and short stories, and has also had articles on bipolar self-management published. She leads a Birmingham-based writing group and occasionally performs her poems at open mic nights. Website: www.janmccarthyauthor.com

Jacqueline Pemberton has been writing poetry for many years and is an active member in local poetry groups and open mics in Lancashire. Jacqueline has previously taught English and now she volunteers as a befriender for Age UK and for The Reader Charity. A number of her poems have been published and she has self published her own poetry collection and cd.

Jean O'Brien is the author of five collections, the most recent being 'Fish on a Bicycle' (Salmon Pub). She has won awards for her work including the Arvon International Poetry competition (2010). She holds an M.Phil in creative writing from Trinity College, Dublin (Irl.) and she currently teaches creative writing in places as diverse as schools, community groups, prisons and the Irish Writers Centre. www.jeanobrien.ie

Jeel Chung (Jeleen Tycangco) is a Philippine based writer aspiring to become a hybrid of a mermaid and a dragon, however life happened and she pursued a career in Engineering. If she is not crunching numbers and data, she is pouring out her heart to poetry and for her passion in sharing her advocacy. You can find out more at her Instagram: @jeelcheng

Jennie E. Owen has won competitions and has been widely published online, in literary journals and anthologies. She is a University Lecturer of Creative Writing and lives in Mawdesley, Lancashire with her husband and three children.

Jeremy Mifsud is a twenty-three year old psychology student from Malta. During a two-year phase of depression, poetry was vital to channel his emotions in a healthier way. Writing became a therapeutic method that worked wonders for his mental health. Even though almost 4 years passed since then, Jeremy has kept poetry as a main tool for expression. Jeremy also engages in mindfulness meditation, writes poetry every day and post some poems on his site as well as work on self-publishing projects.

Jinny Fisher is a member of Wells Fountain Poets. Print and online publications include The Interpreter's House, Under the Radar, Prole, Tears in the Fence , Ink Sweat & Tears and The Poetry Shed. Her poem 'Transition' won 2nd Prize in The Interpreter's House competition, 2016. She likes to push around her Poetry Pram, particularly at poetry and rock festivals. https://www.facebook.com/PoetryPram/

Jonathan Humble is a deputy head teacher in Cumbria. His poems have appeared in a number of publications online and in print, including Ink, Sweat and Tears, Obsessed With Pipework, Atrium, Riggwelter, Amaryllis and Fair Acre Press. My Camel's Name Is Brian, his collection of light poetry, is published by the Tripe Marketing Board.

Jonathan Taylor is an author, lecturer, editor and critic. His books include the memoir Take Me Home: Parkinson's, My Father, Myself (Granta, 2007), the novel Melissa (Salt, 2015), and the poetry collection Musicolepsy (Shoestring, 2013). He directs the MA in Creative Writing at the University of Leicester.

Judith Carmody is a CPA (Certified Public Accountant) from Co Kerry, Ireland. She is a published Author and Poet. She completed a foundation in counselling and a research thesis in communication. She has recently published Co-Bully No More and co-authored FINDING YOUR VOICE: The Assertive & Empowered Woman.

Kathryn Metcalfe has been published in several anthologies and literary magazines. She is a member of the Mill Girl Poets, a group of women who wrote and performed a stage show about the lives, loves and heritage of the Paisley Thread Mill workers. She also founded and runs a monthly poetry/spoken word open mic session in a local coffee shop.

Katie Lewington has been writing ever since she can remember, developing her unique style of writing. She has self-published several chapbooks of poetry on her travels, experiences of love, and humorous food themed pieces too. She works on her blog The Poetry Hub reviewing books, sharing poetry, and interviewing writers. She likes to engage with other writers and bibliophiles through social media.

Kelsi Rose is a Central Pennsylvania-based Poet stuck in her own head who has, for the past twelve years, crafted poetry that caters to a range of emotions, people, and personalities. Her first collection, 'Sparrow' debuted in early 2016 from Winter Goose Publishing, who will also be publishing her second collection at an undisclosed date. Additionally, Kelsi Rose's writing has appeared in Eskimo Pie and is forthcoming in 'Heart of Courage', an anthology coming from Swyer's Publishing Summer 2018. As a person who has struggled with various mental health issues over the past decade, Kelsi Rose understands the importance of mental wellbeing and has often used her writing as a coping mechanism.

Kim Goldberg is the author of seven books of poetry and nonfiction. She is a winner of Canada's Rannu Fund Poetry Prize for Speculative Literature and other distinctions. Her poems have appeared in magazines and anthologies around the world. She lives on Vancouver Island, Canada. https://pigsquash.wordpress.com/

Kitty Coles has been widely published in magazines and anthologies. She was one of the two winners of the Indigo Dreams Pamphlet

Prize 2016 and her debut pamphlet, Seal Wife, was published in 2017. www.kittyrcoles.com

Laura Ashley has been writing since she was in Middle school and became a lot more active with writing in her 20s. Poetry collection 'Table for One' was released in May 2017. Through writing Laura has learned so much and through the writing community. Suffering from anxiety and Multiple Sclerosis, Laura is no stranger to mental health lows but hopes her words will remind others that they are not alone in the fight.

Leila Tualla is a Filipino-American memoirist, poet, and Christian author. Leila's books include a YA Christian contemporary romance called, Love, Defined and a memoir/poetry collection called 'Storm of Hope: God, Preeclampsia, Depression and me'. Her poetry is featured in two mental health anthologies, 'Letters of May' and 'We are Not Alone: Stories of Mental Health Awareness'. She is currently working on a poetry collection based on Asian American stereotypes, titled the Token Asian writes. Leila lives in Houston, Texas with her first generation Mexican American husband and two miracle "Mexipino" babies.

Lexi Vranick is an independent poet and fiction author based in New York. She is the author of 'Ready Aim Fire: A Poetry Collection', 'Basket Case: A Short (Short) Story Collection', and 'Exit Ghost'. She is a member of the Long Island Writer's Guild and a student at Gotham Writer's Workshop. She can often be seen at local book shops, searching for stories at the bottom of coffee cups.

Linda M. Crate has been published in numerous anthologies and magazines both print and online. She is a two-time push cart nominee and the author of four published chapbooks. The latest book of poetry being 'My Wings Were Made to Fly.' (Flutter Press, September 2017).

Lorraine Carey is an Irish poet and artist. Her poems have featured in: The Blue Nib, Ariel Chart, Sixteen, Olentangy Review, The Honest Ulsterman, Proletarian, Poetry Breakfast, Atrium, Poethead, Live Encounters, Three Drops From A Cauldron and Picaroon among others. She has poems forthcoming in Prole, The Runt Zine and Laldy. A runner up in both the Trocaire / Poetry Ireland Competition and The Blue Nib Chapbook Competition 2017, she has contributed poetry to several anthologies.

Margaret O'Driscoll is a full time carer of a loved one with mental health issues and is a poet, editor and curator. She published her first poetry collection in 2016 and it has received star reviews. Many of her poems appear in journals, and magazines worldwide and her poetry is translated into many languages.

Martin Swords is a member of Wicklow Writers Group. He runs Glendalough Guided Walks, giving Walks 'n Talks in the Monastic City and The Valley of Glendalough. He has a background in Communications, Radio and Graphic Design. He has been writing Poetry and short stories since 1990. Martin is published in Lifelines New and Collected, Voyages, Wicklow Writers Anthology, A View from Tiglin, The Space Inside, Wicklow Arts Magazine, Anniversary Anthology celebrating Ten Years of Wicklow Writers; The Prairie Schooner Ireland Edition Winter 2011, University of Nebraska U.S.A., New York Times Blog, and various editions Glendalough and Laragh News. He lives in Tiglin, Co. Wicklow

Melissa Jacob is passionate about inclusion and storytelling. She's most inspired when considering how the latter can facilitate the former. More of her words can be found here: https://sarsaparilla72. wordpress.com/author/sarsaparilla72/

Michelle Diaz has been writing since the late 90s. She has been published by Prole, Live Canon and Amaryllis. She was recently awarded 3rd place in the Mere Literary Poetry competition. She runs a monthly poetry group in Glastonbury. Poetry is her passion.

Mike Gallagher is an Irish writer, poet and editor. His prose, poetry, haiku and songs have been published throughout Europe, America, Australia, Nepal, India, Pakistan, Thailand, Mexico, The Philippines, Japan and Canada. His writing has been translated into Irish, Croatian, Japanese, Dutch, German, Italian and Chinese. He won the Michael Hartnett Viva Voce competition in 2010 and 2016, was shortlisted for the Hennessy Award in 2011 and won the Desmond O'Grady International Poetry Contest in 2012. His poetry collection 'Stick on Stone' was published by Revival Press in 2013.

Melissa Jennings is an English Literature student at the University of Glasgow. They published their debut poetry collection Afterlife in May 2017 and published their first chapbook dear judas in February 2018. Melissa is an avid reader, writer, and reviewer. They are currently working on their next full-length poetry collection, Underworld, which will be released in summer 2018. You can find out more at melissajennings.co

Miriam Calleja is a bilingual author from Malta. Her poetry collections, 'Pomegranate Heart' (EDE Books, 2015) and 'Inside Skin' (EDE Books, 2016), have been described as 'fresh', 'intimate', and 'sensual'. In 2015 she was shortlisted for a literary excellence award for her poem 'Burying the Dark', which has been published in an anthology by Magic Oxygen in the UK. She dedicates her time facilitating creative writing workshops, writing for performances or publications, and devouring books. She has read at events in Malta, London, and New York. In 2017 she was recognised by the Network of Young Women Leaders as a leading female artist in Malta. She moonlights as a pharmacist, loves the sea, cats, coffee, and travelling.

Molly Frawley is a poet from Fife who writes primarily about love, sex, and mental health. Whilst studying in Glasgow, Molly discovered the wonders of spoken word poetry and maintains it is the best form of therapy she has ever experienced.

Nancy Matchton Owens, AKA Nancy Dawn Hails, is from Long Island NY. She is a singer/entertainer/ writer living in Dublin, Ireland. She facilitates a writing group in the community and has co-written a play called 'How safe are your secrets?', performed in Dublin. She writes short stories and poetry and has been published in The Womans Way. At present she is in the process of putting a blog together called Butterflyblues and a lot of the pieces will be surrounding Mental health and well being.

Neil Elder has had work published in a number of magazines and journals. In November 2017 his chapbook, 'Being Present', was published by The Black Light Engine Room and his pamphlet, 'Codes of Conduct', was a winner of the Cinnamon Press Pamphlet Competition. Neil's full debut collection, 'The Space Between Us' is to be published in Spring 2018 with Cinnamon Press. Neil lives in NW London where he teaches at a secondary school.

Niall O'Connor is an internationally published poet and blogger, Pushcart Prize nominee, and author of acclaimed poetry collection 'Change in the Wind'. He now lives in Bunaterin, in Ireland, caught between an ancient Esker and a modern highway. He draws inspiration from both. 'We are invited into a world where humans live in intimate contact with the earth, sea, and sky—where the elemental and its ancient mysteries and deep truths take precedence over the ego-based jockeying and maneuvering of cities.'

Nina Lewis is published in a range of anthologies including Paper Swans Press and Fair Acre Press, magazines including Abridged, Under the Radar, HCE and online. Nina's poems appeared on the Poetry Trail at Wenlock Poetry Festival and BIG Lit Festival, 21 Haiku were used in an Art Installation at the MAC. In 2014 she was commissioned to perform at Birmingham Literature Festival. Her début pamphlet 'Fragile Houses' was published by V. Press, 2016. In 2017 Nina was in Room 204 Writer Development programme- WWM, appointed Worcestershire Poet Laureate and Reader in Residence at Rugby Library -WMRN. Website: https://awritersfountain. wordpress.com/

Olivia Tuck lives in Wiltshire with her parents, her sisters and her Cocker Spaniel – and with Asperger's Syndrome and borderline personality disorder! She was a 2014 Wicked Young Writers' Award finalist, has had pieces published on Amaryllis Poetry, on Lonesome October Lit and in Three Drops from a Cauldron, and recently had a story shortlisted for the Hysteria Writing Competition. Olivia was thrilled to be a guest poet at the 2017 Swindon Poetry Festival. She is due to start at Bath Spa University in the autumn, to study for a BA in Creative Writing.

Owen Gallagher has previously published: 'Sat Guru Snowman', Peterloo Poets, 'Tea with the Taliban', Smokestack Books, and 'A Good Enough Love', Salmon Poetry, Ireland, 2015, which was nominated for the T.S.Elliot award.

Peadar O'Donoghue is the Co-editor of PB poetry magazine, his second collection, The Death of Poetry, is due out in the Spring, from Salmon Poetry. He has been on medication for depression for the past 9 years.

Peter Adair is a 12NOW (New Original Writer) with Lagan Online. He won the 2015 Translink Poetry Competition and the 2016 Funeral Services Northern Ireland Poetry Competition. His poems have appeared in The Honest Ulsterman, The Galway Review, FourXFour, Snakeskin, I am not a silent poet and other journals and e-anthologies. He has read at the Belfast Book Festival and Aspects Festival. He is a member of Queen's University Writers' Group. He lives in Bangor, Northern Ireland.

Peter Lilly is a twenty nine year old British poet who grew up in Gloucestershire. After studying Theology in London, he worked for a homelessness charity in Watford for 5 years where he had the privilege to work alongside 'Mind'. He now lives in Montpellier, France, and has been published in the online journal Barehands. Blog: http://peterlillypoetry.blogspot.com/ Twitter: @peterlillypoems

Peter Raynard is a poet and editor of Proletarian Poetry: the poetry of working class lives, which has featured over 130 poets (www.proletarianpoetry.com). He is a member of Malika's Poetry Kitchen. His poems have appeared in a number of publications and his debut collection, 'Precarious' will be published in April by Smokestack Books. He can be found twittering @peter_raynard; @proletarian_poet

Rachel Burns has been widely published in UK literary magazines. She was shortlisted for The Keats- Shelley Adult Prize 2017. Currently, she is an Arvon/Jerwood playwright mentee. Twitter @RachelLBurnsme; Blog https://rachelburnssite.wordpress.com/

Rachel Davies has been published in journals and anthologies, most recently Riggwelter, The North and Beautiful Dragons Press 'Noble Dissent'. She has been a prize winner in several poetry competitions. She co-ordinates East Manchester and Tameside Stanza, is on Poets & Players organising committee. She has an MA in Creative Writing and is working towards a PhD in poetry from MMU. You can read her blog here: racheld1607.com

Rachel McGladdery lives and writes in rural Lancashire, with her 4 children and 3 cats. She has been published both online and on paper, most recently in YorkMix, Prole and Atrium and has an upcoming poem in Riggwelter. She has made a number of poetry films in collaboration with Big Tree Productions.

Rachel Stephanie Akinyi also known as Spontaneous the poet is a Kenyan 'floet', incorporating both spoken word and music in her artistry. She likes to categorize her works as conscious, inspired by experiences with the Almighty. Aside from artistry, she wears many hats, among them being an Assistant Program Officer at Peace Tree Network, an active humanitarian, and a cofounder and artist manager at ANIKA 254.

Raine Geoghegan, MA, is a poet and prose writer. Her poems have been published in print and online in both literary journals and anthologies. In 2017 she read a selection of poems and monologues in a short film about the Roma, hop picking in Herefordshire, to be screened in 2018. She will also be giving live readings alongside the screenings at various venues and events including Ledbury Poetry Festival. One of her Romani poems will be published in Under the Radar magazine in Spring 2018.

Randall Horton retired in 2016 from teaching philosophy at a community college in Houston, Texas, and moved to Derbyshire County, where he now lives and writes. He holds a PhD in Medical Humanities from the University of Texas Medical Branch in Galveston, Texas.

Ravi Naicker was born and raised on the Farm Glen Albyn. He is a retired Teacher, a keen reader and music lover, and an occasional writer of poems. Ravi recently published his anthology of poems entitled, 'Wellington Rings a Bell'.

Roy Moller was born in Edinburgh of Canadian stock, and now lives in Dunbar, East Lothian. Poetry gives him a way to express the ups and downs of living with dyspraxia. His work has been published by the likes of Ink, Sweat & Tears, Anti-Heroin Chic, And More Poems and in the Neu! Reekie! anthology '#UntitledTwo'.

Ruth Aylett lives in Edinburgh where she teaches and researches university-level computing. She was joint author with Beth McDonough of the pamphlet 'Handfast', published in 2016. One of four authors of the online epic Granite University, she performed

with Sarah the Poetic Robot at the 2012 Edinburgh Free Fringe. She has been published by The North, Prole, Antiphon, Interpreter's House, New Writing Scotland, South Bank Poetry, Envoi, Bloodaxe Books, Red Squirrel Press, Doire Press and others.
See www.macs.hw.ac.uk/~ruth/writing.html for more.

Sallyanne Rock lives in Worcestershire, raising two daughters, reading, learning and writing poetry & short fiction. She has recently been published in Ellipsis Zine.

Sarah Evans has had many short stories published in anthologies, magazines and online. Prizes have been awarded by, amongst others: Words and Women, Winston Fletcher, Stratford Literary Festival, Glass Woman and Rubery. Other publishing outlets include: the Bridport Prize, Unthank Books, Riptide, Shooter and Best New Writing. Writing poetry is a more recent venture.
Twitter: @Sarah_mm_Evans

Sarah L Dixon is based in Linthwaite and tours as The Quiet Compere. She has been most recently published in Confluence Medway. Her first book, 'The sky is cracked', was released by Half Moon Press in November 2017. Sarah's inspiration comes from being close to water and adventures with her son, Frank (7).

Sarah Wallis is a poet and playwright based in Leeds. She works with magical realism and a sense of playful observation both in her stage work, poetry, flash fiction and has been published in numerous journals, most recently the Yorkshire Poetry Anthology from Valley Press, Watermarks; For Lido Lovers and Wild Swimmers by the Frogmore Papers and Ellipsis. She has held residencies at West Yorkshire Playhouse and Harrogate Theatre which supported her plays Laridae and The Rain King.

Seanín Hughes is a poet and writer from County Tyrone, Northern Ireland, where she lives with her partner and four children. She has been published in a number of literary journals, including Poethead, Dodging The Rain, Cold Coffee Stand and projects by Lagan Online and A New Ulster. Seanín's influences and interests lie in a vast spectrum of areas, but she has particular interest in themes involving motherhood, mental health and disability of all forms and types.

SM Jenkin was born in Chatham and is an editorial advisor for Confluence magazine. She performs regularly on the Kent Live-lit scene and has had work published in literary publications including: Anti-Heroin Chic, Boyne Berries, Dissonance Magazine, City Without a Head and The Mermaid.
@sajenks42 and https://www.facebook.com/SMJenkinWriter.

Spreken began writing prose and poetry at a young age, but began to focus on poetry in her early teens. She headlined 'Paint it Black', a poetry night in aid of Mental Health Awareness in 2017, and her first collaborative poetry collection with good friend and poet Matt Chamberlain was published in the same year.
Stephen Byrne is a chef and writer originally from Dublin and now lives in Chicago. His debut book 'Somewhere but not Here' was selected by Vinita Agrawal for the RL Poetry Award, 2016 in the international category. He has been published worldwide and writes about food and recipes for the website, This is Galway. Website: http://stephenbyrne.org/

Stephen Watt is Dumbarton Football Club's Poet-in-Residence. His debut collection 'Spit' was published in 2012 by Bonacia Ltd after beating 8,000 entrants to win the Poetry Rivals slam, and follow-up pamphlet 'Optograms' published by Wild Word Press in 2016. Stephen is one half of experimental gothic music/spoken word project Neon Poltergeist, and became the first 'crime poet' to appear at International Crime Literature festival, Bloody Scotland.

Sue Mackrell has been published in Agenda, The Coffee House, Roundyhouse, Poems in the Waiting Room and Riptide, as well as online. She has an MA in Creative Writing from Loughborough University, where she also taught. More of her work can be found on http://www.writingeastmidlands.co.uk/writers-directory/sue-mackrell-2/

Susan Millar DuMars was born in Philadelphia but lives in Galway, Ireland. She is the author of four poetry collections, the most recent of which, 'Bone Fire', was published in 2016 by Salmon Poetry. Her New and Selected will appear in 2019. Susan is the co-founder and organiser of the Over the Edge readings series in Galway. OTE will celebrate its fifteenth anniversary in January, 2018.

Victoria Richards is a journalist and writer. She was 'highly commended' for poetry in the Bridport Prize 2017, shortlisted in the Hysteria UK Writing Competition 2017 and longlisted in the Yeovil Literary Prize 2017. She lives in London where she is writing a novel, short stories and a poetry collection. Victoria was recently longlisted in the Cinnamon Press Debut Poetry Collection Prize 2017.

William Hatchett is a journalist and the editor of a trade magazine, based in London. William studied English and then American literature at the Universities of Bangor (in North Wales) and Paris VIII (St Denis). His love of writing includes a love of form and structure in poetry and art. The project is close to home for William, who has in the past received treatment for mental health. William is a happy father and granddad.